Smooth Sailing:

How to Avoid Storms in Your Ministry

Jerry Wilkins

First Edition

PAGE PUBLISHING, INC.
New York, NY

First originally published by Page Publishing, Inc. 2014

ISBN 978-1-63417-394-0 (pbk)
ISBN 978-1-63417-395-7 (digital)

Printed in the United States of America

Smooth Sailing

Jerry Wilkins

Endorsements and Recommendations

"Just as C. H. Spurgeon's Lectures to My Students is mandatory reading for any serious student in pastoral ministry, so also should Jerry Wilkins' challenging book Smooth Sailing be high on his list."

—Dr. Paige Patterson, President Southwestern Baptist
Theological Seminary, Fort Worth, Texas

"Jerry Wilkins has written a great help for those of us in the ministry! I only wish I could have had it 40 years ago. I look forward to recommending this book to the hundreds of Pastors I speak to every year."

— Dr. Sammy Gilbreath, Director of Evangelism
Alabama Baptist Convention

"Wilkins offers unique insights concerning the storm causing mistakes we make in ministry. He also is a voice of encouragement for those who are struggling through the stormy times."

— Dr. Rick Lance, Executive Director,
Alabama State Board of Missions

"I have read dozen of books regarding practical advice on successful ministry. Jerry Wilkins book is the most practical book on ministry I have read in years. Make sure your pastor has a copy."

— Dr. Mike Shaw, Retired Pastor and former
President of The Alabama State Convention

"Amen! Amen! Amen! Sixty "Amens", one for each of the brief chapters in this book. It is an easy read, chock-full of nuggets of wisdom from Jerry's many years of productive ministry."

— Dr. Dale Huff, Alabama Baptist Convention

Jerry was called into the ministry at age twenty and served churches for forty-nine years. He just retired from twenty-eight years of service as the associational missionary for the Tuscaloosa County Baptist Association. During this time, he worked with eighty-seven churches and more than four hundred pastors and other ministers. Before that, he served as pastor of churches in Texas, Tennessee, and Alabama. Jerry is a graduate of Southwestern Baptist Seminary and Samford University. Wilkins traveled extensively leading conferences on church outreach and growth. Other books include *Marketing Your Sunday School*, *A Practical Guide to Associational Missions*, *Let God Speak When Conflict Arises*, and *The Great Marriage Physician*. He has been married to Carole for forty-eight years, and they have two grown children and one grown granddaughter. Both Jerry and Carole have authored several books together and continue to write in retirement while serving in their local church.

Contents

Introduction: Simple Headwinds, Storms, and the Perfect Storm

Every pastor and minister, and their families, wish for, pray for, and sometimes beg for some smooth sailing in the ministry. Some ministers seem to have smooth sailing always while others continually go through ministerial storms. Then there are those between these two extremes; those who experience just enough storms to make us pray for some smooth sailing from time to time. I am going to address a multitude of threats to smooth sailing in the ministry. You may think some of them are really small mistakes while agreeing with me that others are big mistakes that can cause huge, even perfect storms. Please don't think I'm being judgmental. I hope you won't think I'm picking at small mistakes most ministers make. As a pastor for nearly twenty years, I know how it feels to be picked at and criticized. As an associational missionary, I worked with so many pastors and other ministers, such as ministers of students, of education, of administration, of senior adults, and of college who were going through storms of varying intensities. My desire is to help every minister be aware of the mistakes that can be made that cause storms in the ministry. Every mistake I address is one I have made or I have personal knowledge of someone else making.

There are storms of every size in the ministry. Some are huge like a hurricane and others are as small as a simple headwind. But who needs a storm of any size. Sure, we all make mistakes and most of us experience storms of some degree. So don't feel odd or defective if you do have storms in your ministry. I did when I experienced a storm early in my own ministry. I went to an older pastor friend and shared about my storm and asked him what I should do. I felt defective when he said he wasn't sure because he had never had any real problems like this. I wondered what was wrong with me. Few are those like him, and many are those like me, then and now. I experienced many storms over my forty-seven years of ministry, some because of mistakes I made and some because I faithfully served and obeyed God. With that said, I believe every minister wants to avoid as many storms as possible, for the sake of our ministry, our family, and the kingdom. One dictionary says a *headwind* is a wind pushing in the opposite direction you want to go. As imperfect as we each are, we still should be aware of the things that have the potential to create headwinds or huge storms and avoid them if at all possible. Isn't it much better to have the wind at our back as much as is possible? As we run the race, let's avoid shooting ourselves in the foot!

There is a powerful truth in scripture. There are none perfect, not even one! In Romans 3:23, we all know that Jesus Christ is the only perfect one, and all of us have our sin, our shortcomings, and our failures. The pastor or minister who believes he can do no wrong and make no mistakes is headed for trouble. This minister walks around with his guard down and leaves himself open to attack. I have experienced this as a pastor of eighteen years myself and have observed it in hundreds of other ministers over my twenty-eight years as an associational missionary.

Hear my heart. I have written this book in an effort to keep ministers from making common mistakes that bring storms into the ministry. Again, every storm-causing mistake in this book were ones I either made, saw someone else make, or heard about someone making. The resulting storms varied in their severity and damage from a slight headwind that simply slows us down to the perfect storm where all is lost. I wish for every minister smooth sailing and hope these words of caution will help many steer clear of the storms on the horizon.

If you have made any of these mistakes, be assured that God is in the business of picking us all up when we fall. He delights in forgiving us when we repent. He is very pleased when we guard our lives and avoid making mistakes like these. It may be that these mistakes have never been a danger to you. Be assured Satan is trying his very best to find what mistake he could get you to make. He may be setting his trap presently. Be vigilant, and be aware of his tricks and traps.

Although no one is perfect, a great deal is riding on the minister's ability to be above reproach and not to bring shame or damage to the kingdom or the reputation of other ministers. Although your church members know you cannot be perfect, they need you to be the best you can be. Our Lord expects nothing less.

A Theology of Mistakes in Ministry

The Bible has many examples of mistakes made by those called to serve God and instructions that can be applied to the lives of ministers. Instructions that will help us avoid the storms. Although none of us will be perfect and all will make mistakes, some of us more than others, every minister should strive for perfection and avoid as many mistakes as possible. Why should we make this effort? What motivates us to watch our step, our words, and our actions? What is at stake if we just stumble through our ministry, making mistake after mistake?

First, we have a holy calling. God expects more of his ministers. The standard for all Christians is high, but the standard is even higher for those of us who have accepted and committed to this high, holy calling of the Gospel ministry.

The Lord, our divine boss, watches all we do, we say, and even what we think. He sees our every move and discerns our every thought. Where can we hide from his watchful eye? Where can we hide our sin? How do we cover up our mistakes and the damage they do to the Church and the kingdom? Nowhere and at no time! Some ministers are lucky enough to avoid the storm from a mistake or a sin; others suffer great storms and great loss. For most of us, we experience the pain and damage from storms of different intensities.

The mistakes I address in the simple book have the potential to damage the local church we are called to care for and lead. Some of these mistakes do great damage. I've seen it take years for a local church to recover from the damage done by a storm made by the minister's mistake. Years of evangelism can be damaged. Years of community influence have been sacrificed by the careless minister. The reputation of the church suffers. Future pastors and ministers have to labor under the weight of the broken trust a former minister leaves behind.

Then there are the hundreds, maybe thousands, of Christians who have dropped out of church attendance, changed churches, and even lost faith because of mistakes ministers have made. I meet these people everywhere I go. They are out of church and point back to a minister who made a terrible mistake or the church conflict caused by a mistake made.

Let's not forget the pain and upheaval caused to our spouses and our children. So many PKs (preacher's kids) leave the church forever because of the conflict and the storms they experienced. They see and hear more than you know or are willing to admit. Their trust is shattered. Their opinion of ministers, the church, and even God are changed by the mistakes and the storms that follow the mistakes.

Then I must mention the storms that come to the minister due to the faults and failures of his or her spouse or children. These storms are not the fault of the minister, but he or she must weather them. It may be the spouse's sexual trespasses or bad habits. My heart broke when I saw a pastor friend lose the church position because the spouse was unfaithful to the marriage. This doesn't always result in your having to leave your church, but church people aren't always as understanding as they should be. For this reason, I've included a section for the minister's spouse later in this book.

The minister's children are not perfect, but again, their sins may cause a storm for the minister. We've all heard the comment meant to be humorous, "The pastor's kid is bad because they have to play with the deacon's kids." Whatever the minister's children do should not be charged against the minister, in my opinion. I know hundreds of ministers who taught and trained their children morally and ethically, but many of these children drank, smoked, did drugs, and were active sexually, and lied about all of it. It is sad that the minister must suffer unjustly for the actions of his children. Christians do their best, and still, all our children stand in danger of falling under the devil's spell and into his traps. So ministers experience storms from three different sources: storms of their own making because of their own mistakes and sins; storms caused by their faithful obedience to the Lord, which I will mention later; and lastly, storms that come because of the mistakes made by the minister's spouse or children. In my opinion, the church should rally around the minister whose children have fallen unto sin, just as we expect the minister to come to the aid of church members whose children go astray.

You may wonder why I didn't fill this book with scriptures referencing all the different mistakes a minister can make and the directions God gives us to help us avoid these mistakes. It's because I feel you and the other ministers reading this book know the scriptures that warn of many of these mistakes. We know but ignore or forget! It's not knowing the Word but doing the Word that matters. "Be ye doers of the Word and not hearers only," right? Also many of these storm-causing mistakes are addressed by common sense, not so much a scripture that tells us to do or not do something.

I hope I've made a good case for avoiding the mistakes that bring the storms into your ministry. I hope I've given you ample reason to strive with Paul, who said he was not perfect nor had he attained all but was determined to press on and to do the very best he could do. It is with this in mind I share the following mistakes ministers make which bring storms rather than smooth sailing to their ministry. Please read on with an open mind and know a minister somewhere has experienced a storm because he or she failed to avoid one of these mistakes.

Storms Brought On by the Mistakes Ministers Make

Storm 1: Church Credit Card

Over the years, I have seen several minister friends get in trouble for financial reasons. Sometimes it was not because they did something wrong or dishonest. It was because they did something that people interpreted was dishonest or wrong. Sadly, perception is reality for many people. Too often, some people judge you guilty until you are proven to be innocent. Several times this perception was tied to the minister's use of the church credit card.

In my opinion, here is a hard-and-fast rule: never use the church's credit card for personal stuff unless specifically authorized to do so by the whole church, and even then, I say, avoid it. I personally don't think you should let a church leader, or even a committee, say it is okay. That's a simple rule, but it may save your ministry. If your church has a credit card, don't carry it around with you and be tempted to use it on something personal. Remember, you're spending the church's money when you sign your name to a church credit card charge even if you plan to pay it back. I have seen this get ministers in deep trouble, resulting in a severe storm. Recently, a fine, upright politician had to explain how he intended to pay back the money he charged on a government committee's credit card. It made him look bad, and the doubt it put in people's minds was damaging to his image. You and I as ministers are never so respected that people won't have this type of misunderstanding. Don't be fool enough to think your people would never think you capable of doing something wrong. This mistake and the great storm that follows are more common than you could know. There's not a whole lot more that I will say about this mistake, but I encourage you to avoid the cards like the plague. Stay away from the church's money, and stay away from the church's credit cards even if someone says it's okay.

Storm 2: Family Members

A practice that's not so common is putting family members on the church staff team. It may be the pastor putting a son or a son-in-law on staff as educational minister or student minister or some other position. It may be the hiring of the minister's wife or brother or sister to serve the church in some capacity as an employee. Whatever the family combination, it may or may not be something God leads you to do, but I have seen it lead to trouble more times than not. I cannot think of a time I've seen it work well. I have seen many cases where it did *not* work well.

Why is it a bad idea? When the pastor puts a family member on staff, church members feel they cannot voice concerns about that staff member or employee without offending the pastor. Church members may feel they cannot question the work or leadership of the staff member or employee for the same reason. I, more than once, have heard church members speak critically of a family-run church. It can bring a storm when it is the pastor's family that is perceived as running things.

In addition, if the pastor must question or correct the family staff member or employee, it could negatively affect family relationships and the relationship with his wife who is naturally protective of the family member.

I have seen this practice cause jealousy and conflict between members of the church staff. Nonfamily staff members can feel there is preferential treatment of the family staff member. This may not be true, but perception is reality for these staff members. This can develop into staff conflict, and staff conflict is often the cause of destructive church conflict and a storm that results in pastor or minister removal. This type storm can bring heavy damage to all concerned.

With so many good ministers available, why take the chance of creating these conditions? Most members of the congregation believe the call of a family member is called nepotism in any other setting. I would only do it after much prayer, much family discussion, and a secret ballot call so you feel the full support of the congregation. Even then, because the congregation usually just goes along, I would avoid this dangerous decision. It may seem you are building a good ship, but that ship might be headed into a storm.

Storm 3: Joy

One problem I see too often is that ministers can lose the joy of their ministry. This loss can be the root cause to many possible storms on the horizon. This loss of joy can happen for different reasons, but no matter what causes it to happen, it is a terrible tragedy. I remember teaching a conference when I was much younger. After the conference, an older minister came up to me. He told me he wished he had as much enthusiasm and joy as I did for the ministry. I asked him what happened to his enthusiasm and was shocked at his answer. He said that when I had beaten my head up against a wall for as long as he had, I would lose my excitement and joy also. I'm not sure what I said in response, but I do remember thinking to myself, "I sure hope not." There have been times in my life when I've been discouraged, but there's never been a time in my ministry when I have considered quitting the ministry. No matter what I went through, I always felt joy over my call and the opportunities of ministry.

Whatever you do, keep the joy and enthusiasm. The loss of the same will have an impact on your effectiveness as a minister. I have noted that, more often than not, a congregation will take on the personality of the pastor and other ministers. They seldom, if ever, rise above the enthusiasm and energy of the pastor and other ministers. If ministers are energized and excited about the work of the church, the congregation follows that lead. If you lose the joy and the enthusiasm, if you get down and depressed, the church will also follow your lead. What power of Spirityou have for good or something else!

If you, your wife, or those around you sense you are *losing it*, you should do something. Don't ignore depression. Don't ignore the signs of burnout. Seek to regain the level of joy and enthusiasm you left behind somewhere. Talk to a trusted fellow minister, a counselor, or your doctor. Above all, talk to the Lord who knows all and provides all you need. For now, let me just say, "Don't lose it! If you do, get it back before it's too late" and the dark clouds gather.

Storm 4: Days Off and Vacation Time

I don't know how many ministers I talk to that seem to boast they never get or take an off day, and that they haven't had a vacation in years. It may be great on the ego to think your church cannot survive without your presence, but it may have devastating effects on your own ministry down the road, especially on your spouse and family. Most churches allow their ministers to have one or two days off every week. I remember the rut I got into in my early ministry when I would constantly do work on my days off. One day, as I sat on the couch with my young son, he looked up at me from the couch and asked when I was going to be off again. I looked down at him and said, "Well, son, I'm off today." Without him responding, I could see the disappointment on his face as I looked down at a book in my hand and my briefcase open with calendar and papers everywhere. I might have been off in some form, but it sure wasn't in a form that my son, nor I, could enjoy together. I'd gotten in a habit of working every day of the week. I was doing a great deal of damage in my own life as I moved toward early burnout. I was also doing considerable damage to my children and to my wife. I was laying the foundation for a storm in my ministry. That day, I realized what I was doing. Then and there, I changed my work habits. After that, if we had our vacations cut short by some church emergency or my days off taken by some church situation, I changed my strategy. I came to the point where I realized that if I didn't take charge of my off time and care about my spouse and family, nobody else would. So I began a simple rule. If my off day was interrupted by church work, I would, at that very moment, commit to my family a compensatory day as soon as possible. I usually picked it on the spot and marked it on my calendar while they watched. They always knew that if my off day got interrupted, they could look forward to another off day in the very near future. I did the same with vacations. I determined I would always take my vacation time, whatever was allotted, but if it were interrupted by church business, then I would commit to my family at that time the other days that I would take to compensate both them and myself for the lost vacation. I stopped feeling proud of the fact I worked so hard and long. Don't misunderstand what I said. I worked hard when I worked and gracefully accepted interruptions into my off time, but I worked just as hard to give my spouse and my children (and me) the time away from work the church gave me and we all needed. If I hadn't, I really think a storm was coming.

What about your spouse and children? What about your need for rest and relaxation? Make it a habit to take your days off and to give your family the time they deserve and need. Don't let your spouse and family end up hating the church for always taking you away from them. Take that vacation time! Your church will not collapse while you are away! If it does, you haven't done a very good job with all the time you do spend with your church. Don't let your ego rob you and your family of this precious time away. Neither you nor I are so important, God can't get along without us. Don't forget to take your off days and your allotted vacations!

Storm 5: Time Off

We should be grateful the church or organization for which we work as ministers provides us with adequate time off. That's as it should be. This includes your vacation, your days off each week, and the hours you're not scheduled to work each day. For pastors and other ministers, these lines can sometime become blurred. It is tough when you don't have to punch a time clock and the only person watching your time is God himself. Many ministers who have little supervision get in trouble because they abuse the privilege of taking time off whenever they choose.

It is good for a minister to have set office hours and for the church to know when the minister expects to be working. Expectations are important, and perceptions are reality when it comes to what people think you're doing or not doing. Transparency is the key. Make sure the entire congregation knows when you're normally working and when you're scheduled to be off. As we have said in other places, it is very important to take your vacation time and to observe your all days if not for your own sake for the sake of your family. But if you abuse this time off, playing when you should be working or sleeping when you should be writing and planning or simply goofing off at the mall or a bookstore when you should be out visiting, you may be heading into a storm. I think I too often took liberty and called work time the time I spent at the coffee shop or Internet café talking to friends and others. Many of us rationalize, saying we are touching people when that's not really the case. It is unethical for a minister to take pay for time he is not working. This is a matter of personal integrity. The church not knowing and asking God to sanction or forgive doesn't make it okay. Getting caught in the pattern can bring storm clouds as your people label you as lazy.

I recently heard a member of one congregation complaining their minister scheduled an hour or two for his devotional time in prayer each morning. This dedicated Christian said he does not get the privilege of using an hour or two of his workday for such holy exercise. Evidently, he felt that a minister, like other members of the church, should be doing his personal devotions on his own time and not including them in the work hours the church requires. Whether you think that is true or not, it would do all of us good to think about how we use the time that we're supposed to be working for the church. I know personally that it can become easy to read and do research on the computer (surfing), or read a bunch of magazines and the newspaper, to talk to friends on the phone or text or Twitter, or visit with someone in the mall or browse the bookstore and neglect the real work of the ministry. What is the real work of the ministry? Well, that's a decision each of us will have to make. After making that decision, we must determine how much of our time, our work time, we are spending toward those objectives. Just being busy is not the same as getting the right things done. Don't suffer a ministry storm because you spent too much time doing good and comfortable things to the neglect of the difficult, uncomfortable things.

Storm 6: Organization

One of the problems many ministers face is the inability to organize or structure their work. I run into ministers all the time who keep no calendar. They often miss meetings because they're simply not organized. Disorganization has been the downfall of many a pastor or minister. People may perceive an unorganized minister to be lazy. Flying by the seat of your pants may be comfortable for you, but most successful ministers and other professionals keep a calendar and organize their day. When a minister forgets things, misses meetings, or in some way forgets a ministry project or activity, those who are aware of it begin to see that minister as lazy and/or disorganized. Most people in our churches are involved in secular work, and disorganization and laziness is not easily tolerated there, and they have a hard time accepting it in the kingdom's minister. Here are some suggestions that might help you, as a minister, become more organized?

Keep a calendar and refer to it often. Whether you use a large calendar, a small pocket calendar, or an electronic calendar of some sort, the important thing is that you keep the calendar up to date and refer to it often. Form the habit of looking at your calendar every morning, at midmorning, at noon, midafternoon, and then when you finish your day, think ahead about anything that needs to be done before the evening is over or some preparation for an event the next day or two. (Oh yea, remember to calendar that off time) Continue to look down your calendar several days and weeks. Oftentimes things that go neglected are the things that are done to prepare for an upcoming event or meeting. This is one of the hardest things I have found to do. I try to force myself to look down my calendar further so that I anticipate preparation for upcoming events. I learned the value of calendaring the preparation and promo actions at the same time I calendar the event or meeting itself. Remember, check your calendar often. (I really liked having a secretary who kept me on schedule and later those new gadgets where I could set multiple reminder alarms.) I still remember and cringe when I think about missing that wedding planning session with the bride and groom from two prominent families in my church.

Keep notes on ministries and events. A simple note kept in your calendar or on your desk or in a folder would be greatly helpful in keeping up with multiple projects. Don't depend on scraps of paper in your pocket to manage something as important as your church. Find a system that works for you. If a system fails you, find another system. Make notes of when you contact members of your church. Date those notes so that you know when you talked to a member about what. The same types of notes can be kept on every committee and ministry of your church. If you have a perfect memory, this may not be needed. For most of us who handle multiple projects, we simply suffer with an overload of information. Because of our hectic schedules, much of that information does not lodge itself in our brains so that we can pull it up easily later. The keeping of these notes may keep you out of trouble in the future.

Keep a good record of prospect visitation. It is the easiest thing in the world to forget about and let fall through the cracks prospects for your church. This is also true for the inactive members of your church. Find some system that will let you track your prospects and your contact with those prospects. This can be done through the Sunday school, through a prospect file, or through your own personal file. As a pastor, I found it was essential to keep my own personal file of high-priority prospects. I found the best system was one which would let me glance down through a list of prospects and easily see the last time I had made contact with each one. I tried to keep notes of when I made personal contacts as opposed to telephone, mail, e-mail, or text. Your church members can overlook a lot of things, but overlooking a needed visit to an important prospect can damage your ministry. Too much neglect can bring on a storm. Remember, whether right or not, most members think they pay you to get these contacts made.

Keep yourself organized in your hospital visitation. This would include visiting those who are in the nursing homes and at home shut-ins. Many church members see this as a high-priority responsibility of the church minister. Keep track of these ministry contacts and be ready to show your contact record to persons who question your faithfulness to this difficult task. Keeping a record of this type helps you to not forget about the need to visit a particular person. I have fought this problem all of my ministry, and learning to keep these types of records helped me greatly. Sometimes we become so busy in the everyday work of the ministry, we forget the actual ministry to the people who need it most.

Get organized in a way that works for you, but by all means, get organized to do the many tasks of the modern minister. Those ministers who do not get and stay organized may need to make space for a storm on the calendar they don't use.

Storm 7: Balance

We hear so many voices today. Some say we should major on evangelism, some say discipleship, others say ministry or deeper life, and still others something else. Some major on their work or their ministry as opposed to their family. Others focus on family and personal renewal as opposed to the work of the church. Some preach and teach only from the Old Testament while others only the New Testament. Some only talk about the grace and forgiveness of God to the neglect of the wrath and righteousness of God. Others do just the reverse of that.

On and on we could go. Maybe we ministers get stuck in a rut of our own making. Since all of these things are important and deserve our attention, it seems to me the great need is for balance.

Too many lack the ability to focus on more than one thing at any given time. Examples of emphasis that draw all a minister's energy could include social ministry, Church growth, deeper life. Any emphasis on which the minister spends all his time and energy could be the important issue or ministry that causes the minister to lose balance. Ministerial balance is the ability to have emphasis without the neglect of the other important issues and ministries. A minister with passion for evangelism should not lose touch with the need for social ministry or the need for discipleship ministry. The minister passionate about deeper spiritual life and discipleship should not neglect the need of people to hear about evangelism and soul winning.

What we need is *balance*! A minister must lead his church forward in all the Church's ministries, not just the one the minister enjoys most. The danger of an impending storm comes when the many ministries of the church get neglected to the benefit of the one ministry the minister leader is overly passionate about. The unity of the congregation can give way to budget battles, turf wars, and hurt feelings or feelings of neglect. I have witnessed these and noticed the lack of balance brought trouble.

The key is balance. God has given the church much to do; let's do it all. Let's strive for balance! Lead your church to be involved in evangelism, discipleship, deeper life, social ministry, worship, and all that fulfills the commands of our great God.

God has given every minister passion for some things but also responsibility for many things.

Storm 8: Opposition

I served as a pastor for eighteen years before becoming a denominational leader. In every church I pastored, I had some opposition. Some of that opposition was merited, and much of it, not so much. I've found that a minister, especially a pastor leader, is easily misunderstood and often criticized. Most of us will experience opposition if we are leading the church in any significant way.

The storms come when we do not expect this opposition, and it catches us off guard. Too often, we want to sweep the opposition under the rug, pretending it doesn't exist. This might work for a short period of time, but opposition never goes away just because it is ignored. Opposition, when left unaddressed and left to fester, will usually get worse.

It is best to address opposition honestly and humbly. A minister who is close to God and sure of his calling does not need to run from opposition. Opposition can be confronted in a positive and loving way. We have to remember that different people have different ideas about how things should be done. Let's not expect everyone to agree. Let's have respect for all our people and be open to their ideas and opinions.

In any movement, in any change, leadership should expect to experience some opposition. So when that opposition comes, realize it is an affirmation that you're doing something. Never fall into the trap of believing you can do no wrong or make no mistakes. Use opposition to help you evaluate your leadership and the direction you are going. If after evaluation you believe your course is correct, then address the opposition with love and determination. If you are sure of yourself, be determined to convince the opposition of the wisdom of following your leadership.

The great mistake I am addressing is the tendency to become discouraged when opposition is encountered. You're in good company and in a lot of company. When we don't expect any opposition, we tend to get discouraged, defensive, or even ready to quit on Monday when we do encounter opposition to our leadership.

Expect opposition and use it with God's help to make your ministry more effective.

Storm 9: Criticism

Criticism is a part of the ministry. Take heart in this fact: every minister will receive criticism. Some may say they don't, but they were just not listening. Criticism is not all justified, but if we were honest, we might find a little bit of truth in any criticism. The key is to be accepting of your own humanity and your own ability to make mistakes. If you can do this, you can handle criticism much better. Can I share with you a few pointers which helped me in the way I manage criticism in my life?

Look at criticism as helpful. Allowing others to share helpful criticisms can make you a better person. It can keep you from repeating mistakes and give you insights you might not have otherwise.

Express openness to criticism. Tell others, even your congregation that you welcome constructive criticism. Don't discourage criticism by getting angry or depressed when criticism comes. This will cause others to withhold valuable suggestions that may be helpful. Others see us differently than we see ourselves, and we need their perspective from time to time.

Thank the one who criticizes you. This shows good self-esteem and your openness to criticism. This would encourage kinder criticism and will disarm those who seek to hurt you by criticism.

Ask for a criticism from time to time. Every now and then, ask for some constructive criticism. Ask for the opinion of someone else in front of other people. This creates a positive atmosphere for honest communication. This openness can actually reduce the criticism in the long run.

Respond positively to criticism. You do this by *what you say* and *what you do* when criticism comes. Always respond by saying you will think about the suggestion. You could actually change something if you determine the criticism is valid. If you do, thank the one who helped you see the need for a change of some kind. Then publicly give that person credit for the good advice.

Finally, accept the fact that you *cannot* do everything others want of you. You cannot be everything others want you to be. Change what you can. Do what you can. And what you cannot change or don't want to change, accept. Ask others to except it also. Talk about it with those who want you to change. Talking about and explaining changes you cannot or will not make can actually improve the relationships. Others may follow your example and be open to criticism. Others may become more willing to change themselves. Relationships will survive and grow when people manage criticism better. Look out! Here comes a criticism. How will you respond?

Storm 10: Demons

As ministers of the Gospel and leaders in the church of Jesus Christ, we can easily convince ourselves we are all on the side of right, on the side of God all the time. It's hard for us to believe what we feel or think could be wrong. It's hard for us to believe we should have any opposition. When we do have opposition, we tend to demonize it. Surely if we're on the side of God and right, anybody that opposes us must be on the side of Satan and are wrong. We see the opposition as evil, and we tend to discount their opposition because we believe it's of the devil.

How can we be so naïve? How can we be so narrow-minded, or should I say, close minded. How have we come to believe we have such a connection with God that we can never make a mistake and never read God's will wrongly?

It is a mistake to think like this. Your opposition as a minister may be of the devil and, then again, it may not. To be honest, I now believe there were times in my ministry when the opposition was pointing me toward a better understanding of God's will. Sometimes my opposition helped me see a different point of view or a better way. Now I think the opposition should have been considered angels because they were helping me avoid a terrible pitfall.

I guess what I'm trying to say here is don't automatically assume that anyone who is against you is of the devil. At least withhold that judgment until time and circumstance prove it to be the case. For sure, avoid openly saying your opposition is of the devil. If you do so, you may force people to take sides. You may then be demonizing some very good people who have good intentions. It is easy for a minister to lose credibility simply because he takes this easy road away from criticism. Some ministers actually create a storm in their attempt to avoid a storm.

Often, this is because the minister has never really learned to deal with conflict in the proper way, the biblical way. I believe some of us forget or ignore everything we have learned from God's word about how we are to act when conflict arises. The word of God is very clear as to how we are to speak, act, and react as Christians. These instruction are not cancelled or to be disregarded just because we are engaged in some type of conflict. But in spite of this, too many Christians might as well toss God's word out the window when we are in conflict. Sadly, some ministers model for others this mismanagement of conflict. I say that because too many of us totally ignore God's commands when we feel the heat of conflict. So what does God say about how all Christians, especially ministers, should act during a conflict.

The Christian life is to exhibit the fruit of the spirit (Gal. 5:22). This includes self-control. We can only control ourselves, and that control is very important in times of conflict. That control can influence others and change the path conflict takes. Ministers should never have to say, "I just lost it" or "I just lost control of myself," or "I forgot how I should act because I was upset."

Even when in conflict, we should always speak the truth in love (Eph. 4:15). God commands us to always speak truth, not falsehoods, not gossip, not inaccurate information or rumor. Words like "you always, you never, you are of the devil," or "you don't love your church" may come out of our mouths but not be the *truth*. We should be careful we always speak the truth and to do it in a loving way with a loving motive. This brings me to the next command we too often ignore when in conflict and dealing with people who oppose us.

As difficult as it is at times, we are to always be kind to others (Eph. 4:32). We are told this several times in God's word, so it must be important. When you think the opposition is of the devil, do you justify your unkind words and actions? Do we demonize those who oppose us so that we can feel good acting in the flesh and being anything but kind?

We are to cease from anger (Eph. 4:31). We are told by God to let all bitterness, and wrath, and *anger*, and clamor, and evil speaking, be put away from us with all malice. God's word says, "But now ye also put off all these; anger, wrath, malice, blasphemy, filthy communication out of your mouth" (Col. 3:8). We can't deny that God's word says that man's anger is always bad and is to be put away and avoided. The assertive actions of Jesus in the temple cannot be equated with the human anger. It is sin and to be avoided like all the other sinful things mentioned just above. God's wrath and the temple anger we like to reference to, to justify our angry human outburst do not give us the freedom to engage in being angry at the opposition. Put it away!

We are to resist the urge to retaliate or get back at someone we demonize. Jesus said we were to turn other cheek, the opposite of retaliation. "Avenge not yourselves, but rather give place unto wrath: for it is written, Vengeance is mine; I will repay, saith the Lord" (Rom. 12:19).

We are to work toward peace. God's word says that God is not the author of confusion but of peace.

We are to be peacemakers waging peace not war, forgiving, not getting revenge.

We are to observe all God's submission principles. We are good at telling people that these guidelines include the relationships between mankind and the earth, citizens and government, slaves(employees) and masters(employers), children and parents, wives and husbands, Christians and their leader-ministers, and Christians and the Lord God. But God goes on to honor his submission principles as he instructs all of us to be in submission to each other in a Spiritof humility. God puts a great value on humility and expects us to exhibit it at all times even when we are dealing with opposition.

Notice that all the above applies also to the chapters on opposition, criticism, and anger as well as to the times we demonize the opposition.

Before I conclude this section, let me say one last thing. We must recognize the role Satan plays in conflict of any kind. First Peter 5:8–9 says, "Be sober; be vigilant, because your adversary the Devil stalks about seeking who he can devour. Resist him, steadfast in the faith" Ephesians 4:27 says, "Nor give place (opportunity) to the devil." Ephesians 6:11 says, "Put on the whole armor of God, that you may be able to stand against the wiles (schemes) of the devil." Second Corinthian 2:11 says, "Lest Satan take advantage of us, for we are not ignorant of his devices." First Timothy 3:7 says, "Less we fall into the snare (trap) of the devil." Galatians 5:19 says, "Now the works of the flesh are evident, hatred, contentions(strife), wrath (anger), dissentions (arguments),selfish ambitions (desiring your way). James 3:14–15 says, "If you have bitter envy and self-seeking in your heart, this wisdom (way of thinking) does not descend from above (God) but is earthly… demonic (of the devil)."

Satan loves to set traps for the minister. Satan loves to draw him or her into conflict, and all the evils that can result from the minister's inability or refusal to do all things God's way. When we get in the flesh, our members and church leaders see it, and this can bring the storms. I've seen this often. I pray you will stay in the Spiritand turn away from the devil's temptation to act in the flesh and the ways of your old man.

Storm 11: Church Money

In one of my early pastorates, one of my church leaders, who was responsible for handling the morning offerings, walked out the front door and laid the bag of offerings in my hands. He was mad because of the decision I had made about the way they had handled the mission offering under the leadership of his son, who was pastor just before me. The minute that money hit my hand, I remembered what I had been taught by one of my wise professors at seminary. He told the entire class they should never, under any circumstances, have the offerings or any other money of the church in their possession. I quickly called over one of the other deacons and handed the money off to him, telling him to not do anything until another deacon was with him to verify anything they did with the money.

It is a wise minister who stays away from the church's financial books and other financial records as well as the money. It is a wise minister who can never be accused of taking or mismanaging funds that belong to the Lord and his church. This is one area we should be very careful. We are to avoid any appearance of evil. Whether you do anything wrong or not, you open yourself up to accusations and the storms that follow. A storm of a financial nature can destroy your ministry. As we have said elsewhere in the book, avoid any personal use of credit cards that belong to the church. Be very careful in the use of petty cash if it is available to you. Make sure every expenditure has a paper trail that protects you from any accusation. Any expenditure for which you should receive reimbursement should be supported by a receipt or a signed document explaining what and when and where and why you spent the money. You don't have to do anything wrong to be accused of doing something wrong.

Your ministry is far more valuable than any money you could handle. Any control you feel you need over the finances of the church is ill desired in light of the storm that could result. Build a good relationship with your finance or budget committee, your treasurer, and anyone else that handles the money of the church. Explain to them why you are going to avoid this mistake. They will understand, and they will appreciate you all the more. None of them want to see any storms over financial issues.

Storm 12: Appreciation

I have often heard someone say that they left the church because they just did not feel appreciated. I've often talked to church leaders and workers who continue to serve but expressed terrible disappointment in the fact that they seldom heard a word of appreciation.

Ideally, we're not supposed to expect appreciation or applause. As Christians, we are to work unselfishly, not expecting anything in return, especially a word of gratitude or appreciation. I'm not sure this is entirely true. I wonder if it makes good sense to lose good church members simply because we are too lazy or too impersonal or too busy to express appreciation in some way. And what a shame so many labor for the Lord without ever feeling appreciated by others. This lack of appreciation may not cause a storm like the ones we've been talking about, but this lack of appreciation does cause a storm of negative emotions that then negatively affect our ministries and our churches.

My experience has been that when you express appreciation, it is not only good for you but for everyone and everything. I believe ministers should create an atmosphere of appreciation and applause. In the book of Acts, Barnabas was called the encourager. Maybe we would do better as church ministers if we encourage those who worked in the church through expressions of appreciation. Here are some suggestions as to how you might begin or maybe just improve the way you express appreciation.

Sit down and make a list of those whom you appreciate. After you make the list, keep the list on your desk until you have expressed appreciation in some way to every person on that list. Keep the list on your desk and add to that list additional people that you decide you should express appreciation to. That list will become a reminder to help you as the minister encourager to daily express appreciation to one or two people every day. Mark the list each day with the record of those you expressed appreciation to that day. My system included a column for the name, phone number, address, e-mail, and then empty columns where I placed the date and method of my communication of appreciation.

Use a variety of creative ways to express appreciation to those on the list. Consider a handwritten note, a thirty-second phone call, a text message, or an e-mail. Make a personal visit or call attention to someone from the pulpit on Sunday morning. Once you get going, you'll be amazed at how many different ways you can find to say thank you. The list helped me touch everyone eventually and to give a little time each day to this simple habit that meant so much to so many. I often got a note of appreciation for my note of appreciation. Wow! I felt like these short communications were making so many people smile and feel better about themselves. I averaged about a minute or two for each call, note, e-mail, or text. And I felt I got a big return for such a small investment.

You never know, in this atmosphere of appreciation, someone might even say thank you to you. You never know, one day your congregation may express appreciation for all you do. Don't be guilty of craving the appreciation of others and not be one who showers his or her world with the same. Don't let anyone leave your church because they felt unappreciated. Don't watch anyone resign a position because he or she didn't feel appreciated.

Storm 13: Delegation

It is one crazy minister who thinks he can do everything or that he or she is the only one that can do anything right. Those are two reasons so many ministers fail to delegate. There's so much to the ministry today that we need to delegate responsibility to others in order to get the work done. Small storms can result from your unwillingness to delegate. If you have the feeling that you're the only one that can do something right, realize there was a time when you were not even around and there will come a time when you won't be around anymore. Failure to delegate may be the height of egotism. Think about all of the things you do every day. Maybe you need to do all of those things or maybe you don't. Maybe there are things you don't get done that you could get done if you would simply delegate more responsibilities to others.

If you're going to delegate, make sure you give the person you delegate a responsibility to the freedom to accomplish the task in their own way. It may not be so important that the results look exactly as you want them to look or that they got done exactly the way you wanted them to get done. God's kingdom tends to survive even when things aren't done perfectly or the way we want them to be done. Give people the freedom to get it done in the best way they know how to get it done.

Remember, good delegation always includes clear expectation and inspection. And delegation requires some follow-up. Follow up to inspect the work of somebody you delegated a task to, checking to see if the work is getting done. Don't assume anything! It's okay to follow up after a period of time to make sure that the task has been completed. But if you delegate well, you will find yourself able to get more accomplished as a minister. Remember that the work of the minister is to equip the saints for the work of the ministry, and delegation is a great way to do just that.

Oh yes, don't forget to express that appreciation to the ones to whom you delegate!

Storm 14: Vision

Over the years, I have seen storms develop for pastors as a result of no vision logically followed by no leadership and the church drift that follows. I believe God send every pastor or minister a vision of what he wants accomplished. A minister has to first be open and receive that vision. The minister may then have that vision in his own heart and mind. He should clearly understand what the vision is *before* he seeks to communicate that vision to other leaders and to his congregation. To move too quickly and share a vision that is not clear in your own mind may doom the real vision to failure. One important principle of leadership is the principle of having and effectively communicating vision. Ministers seeking to lead the church in the twenty-first century must have a vision and *communicate* that vision. It is true that without vision, the people perish. This truth should be applied to the local church. The people of God are admonished to dream dreams and have visions of what God wants to do in the future. Churches and their leaders must constantly envision what God is seeking to do in and through the church. But once the vision becomes clear to some, it can be lost because of the inability to communicate that vision effectively. The result may be going nowhere or just wandering around as a church.

Many ministers are proactive and have great vision for the church they lead. This vision is essential if a church is to move forward. It is important to *define* the vision. The minister defines the vision by first writing it down. Write down in your own words what you believe the vision is. Now edit that vision and refine the vision by clarifying and simplifying it. Always check that the vision you believe God has given you is in accord with his word. Take out unnecessary parts of the vision, if it does not hinder the content of the vision itself, in order to simplify the vision. Clarify the vision by looking for words that are too complicated or statements that do not communicate well with people who are not in the ministry.

Now move in the opposite direction. Think the vision through all its phases and to its ultimate fulfillment. As you do, list the necessary steps, the barriers along the way, and the ultimate results of the vision once fulfilled.

You may share all of the above with some friend or fellow minister who will help you see it even more clearly. Be open to constructive suggestions. A vision that is too fragile for this scrutiny may never stand the test of time as you present it to your congregation. This step has saved me from embarrassment, the loss of face, and the loss of confidence from the congregation.

Remember, once you share your vision with the entire congregation, you risk something. You run the risk that the congregation will not follow the vision or that the vision will not produce the results you had envisioned. A good leader is willing to risk in order to be proactive and to move the church forward through a vision. Too often, a Christian leader will fail to share his vision out of fear people will not follow his vision. This is to deny the essence of leadership. The ability to inspire people toward a visionary goal and to motivate those people toward the sacrifice needed to achieve their goals and objectives is true leadership. If the leader does not have the ability to risk, he may not have the ability to be a visionary leader. Many leaders slide into a reactive leadership role rather than a proactive role simply because of the fear of failure. They chose to do what the people too often drift into doing, rather than dream the dreams and have the visions.

A God-given vision will stand the test and will only be refined through this process of evaluation.

Storm 15: Communication of Your Vision

The wise minister will give as much attention to the effective communication of the vision as to the vision itself. Once the vision is received, the challenge of communication faces the visionary. How do you communicate your vision with the people who are going to help bring the vision to pass? How do you share your dreams in such a way that the dreams become reality in the days ahead? The inability to properly communicate your vision with other leaders and the congregation can often destine your dreams to failure. Many great visionaries fail to move forward for God simply because they have not learned to effectively communicate their vision. Let's look at a process through which the minister can communicate the vision God has given him. Again, the lack of vision or the inability to effectively communicate your vision may create an atmosphere where storms develop.

Make the vision visible. It is important that the vision become visible to the leadership and eventually the entire congregation. The ultimate goal is to adopt the vision as a congregation. This best comes after some process of long-range planning or presentation to the appropriate group that can recommend the vision to the congregation. There is strength in numbers. This approval process in itself may be only the first step in making the vision visible to the congregation. Be careful not to rush this process! Adding more people to the defining of the vision clarifies and purifies the vision and gives you a test run with the smaller group. If you can't sell a few, you can't sell the many. Take your time. Don't rush this process. If it fails to get approval the first time up, it is difficult to lead people to consider it a second time. Make sure you take adequate time to sell to other leaders and to those who will present or recommend the vision. Your congregation may need to be conditioned to receive the vision just as you were.

Once accepted, it is important to keep the vision before your people in every way possible. Make sure they understand the vision and the implications of every phase of the vision. Help them understand what this vision will require of the church family and of the leadership. The questions you fail to answer will be asked by someone somewhere along the way. Answer those questions in your unveiling or your constant presentation of the vision and all its parts.

Put the vision in its simplest form and post the vision in as many places as feasible. You can use your church newsletter, Sunday bulletin, bulletin boards, walls, space over water fountains, restrooms, etc. Posters and banners can also be used to get parts of the vision visibly displayed. It is not necessary to share the entire vision each time. You may zero in on specific parts of the vision from time to time and in different places. If the vision logically falls into three steps, make visible each step as its implementation draws near.

The effective minister learns to share the vision often. Remember, people tend to forget. Often times, they work at forgetting. The wise minister will consider sharing the vision in *sermon* form. Sermons are effective in raising the commitment level of the congregation in the many areas the vision requires. Repetition is so important. People tend to forget tomorrow what you shared with them yesterday. A series of sermons may help make the various parts of the vision more understandable. Remember, only a portion of the full congregation hears the material each time. Another group over really hears it the third time you say it. Don't be afraid of repetition. You can say the same thing in many different ways. Between these sermon reminders, the minister can use the newsletter, Sunday bulletin, and mail outs, and other special means available today, to again talk with the congregation about the vision. You might address the *biblical basis* for the vision in one article while you address the *requirements* of the vision in another. In still another, you might look at the wonderful *results* of the vision while, in another, you might address the *barriers* to achieving the vision. Using all these methods, it will be easy to keep the vision in front of your people in some form every two or three weeks. In this way, the vision becomes a household word. When you mention it, almost everyone knows what you are talking about. Special seminars help you share vision with a select group of leaders or with the entire church family. In my last two pastorates, I remember taking the Sunday night training hour for a period of about twelve weeks. Every adult was invited to attend for a special seminar which would explain the vision for our church and how to achieve that vision. It was interesting to watch people become interested in the achieving of a dream. Not everyone bought in, but enough did to move the church forward. The vision was of such high visibility that few were willing to risk opposing the vision because it seemed to be so well accepted by the majority of the congregation.

There are certain leaders who need to become part to the visionary team. These may include other ministerial staff members, deacon leadership, key leaders of programs in your church and, of course, your Bible teachers. All of these are equally important, but some are more effective in sharing the vision with the congregation than others. Often times, teachers of Bible study classes, once they buy into the vision, become your best promoters of the vision. So look for opportunities to share the vision, specifically with your teachers.

It is important that you never assume that they fully understand or that they will remember. Rather, assume that people understand less than we think and forget much more than we think. Again, I cannot over emphasis the importance of *repetition*. It is wise to calendar the presentation of your vision over a period of a month or so. Write each step down on your calendar. Plan when and how you are going to mention it then step back and look at the calendar from a long-range perspective. Ask yourself, "Is this enough?" Do you need more? Do you need to add other channels of communicating the vision? Be creative! Put the vision on a DVD or some other medium available when you read this book (my first draft mentions using cassettes). Maybe do a video, or Internet presentation. What about a special brochure or pamphlet explaining the vision? And print enough for several distributions along the way.

Finally, *evaluate* the actions, expenditures, and strategies in relation to the vision. Constantly evaluate whether or not you are moving toward the vision's objectives. Accountability is a necessary key to success. Everyone must be accountable to someone as to their role in carrying out the vision. You should preplan your evaluation times. This is wise because we often become so involved in maintaining the church program that we tend to forget the vision once it is put into place. Without follow up, visions die. So calendar times to sit down and evaluate all you are doing in light of the vision. This helps you continue to move in the direction of your vision and to say no to the things that would distract you from the direction of the vision. Properly communicated, a *vision* is that which God uses to move a church off complacency and into action. It is vision that God used to move his people from Egypt to the Promise Land. And it is visionary leaders who must stand out in front of people and point the way. Before, after, and all during this process, remember the place of prayer. Without him, you can do, accomplish nothing. Pray as if everything depends on God because, ultimately, it does. Then work as if all depended on you!

Storm 16: Work Ethic

That leads us to this very logical next chapter. There's one interesting thing about the ministry. Most ministers are the masters of their own lives. By that I mean we may work for the Lord, and God may always be watching us, but we have a way of thinking we are our own boss. I have observed that many ministers have a little problem being accountable to anyone about their work. Sometimes a minister can feel that because he works odd hours that he can be off anytime he chooses. This sounds good in theory, but in the real world, other working people frown on this attitude. A storm's acoming as they say. This attitude has gotten many ministers in trouble because church people notice when you're not around. And when you're working, not as much is noticed. It's very important to have your designated days off and your designated vacation time. It's also wise to have set office hours when your church people can know that you are there. When you're out of the office, somebody ought to know how to reach you. The less-than-good work ethic of a few has caused suspicion of the many.

There's a terrible temptation for a minister to become lazy. That laziness may take the form of just sitting at your desk daydreaming or reading the numerous magazines or publications that tempt you to spend hours of time in them. The computer has become a great temptation for many ministers who spend twice as much time in sermon preparation as opposed to being able to do their sermons in half the time. I've already mentioned earlier the coffee shops, Internet café, and that time-consuming book store where you see all your ministry friends.

Please! Understand I am not saying you should work all the time or seldom be off or take a vacation. I do make that clear in other sections. What I'm saying is I've heard so many church people comment on the lazy or unavailable minister. I've seen so many storms caused by the perception that the minister works very little. I'm trying to risk your friendship out of concern for your ministry and your happiness in the ministry.

Be careful that you don't make the mistake of not working your forty hours. I know many ministers think they work fifty, sixty, seventy, and eighty hours a week, and maybe some do. I thought I did! But when I really clocked my hours, they were less than I thought. There is great danger in working too much or too little. Be careful about working at home all of the time. When church members can't see you at work, many will assume you're not working. I love the idea of working at home, but I'm not sure it's a good idea. Just be aware this is one mistake you don't have to make. Have a good work ethic. Work your hours even when no one is looking, and avoid the storms.

Storm 17: People Pleaser

God's word warns us about ministers who have itchy ears. The implication here is that some ministers like to be praised and appreciated for the things that they say and do. And don't we all! They love to get complements and to please the people. This is not a bad trait unless it becomes the controlling force of your ministry. It is okay to have people like you and to receive complements, but when your soul desire is to please the people, you may sacrifice honesty and truth in that pursuit.

Some ministers avoid controversial subjects simply because they do not want to alienate any of their congregation. What subject do you avoid preaching on simply because you don't want to irritate some of your congregation? You don't want to hurt someone's feelings. We could cite the example of failing to preach on habits such as smoking or drinking or overheating or lust or breaking the law by speeding or rolling stops or, well, you tell me.

Much of the Bible does offend and put pressure on us to change our lifestyle. If a minister is not careful, he or she may neglect those commandments and directions that make people uncomfortable. I don't believe very many ministers do this deliberately. There's so much in the Bible to preach anyhow. It's not very hard to simply stay busy preaching the things that do not irritate your congregation as much. I've heard many sermons about biblical history and characters, but few about anger, lust, cheating, sex outside marriage, cohabitation, and the evils of alcohol and drugs. Surely, we're not afraid of not pleasing the people! They may not bring the storm, but maybe God will.

Each minister must evaluate his own preaching content to see whether he may be guilty of neglect certain truths in the scripture because he has a desire to please his people.

This desire to be a people pleaser can also affect your leadership style. A minister may avoid the creation of new ministries or the pushing of important ministries because of the pressure this puts on his congregation. They may shy away from leading the congregation to a deeper level of commitment or a stronger commitment and sacrifice.

I guess the bottom line is whether or not you and I as a minister want to please God or the people we serve. We should remember the strong words Jesus had for the religious leaders of his day. I hope we would all admit is more important to please God in our ministry and to avoid the temptation to be a people pleaser.

Storm 18: The Affair

I believe every minister can think of someone or many someones they have known in the ministry that have fallen prey to an affair. It seems like it has become too common to hear about a minister who has fallen out of the ministry because they have fallen into an affair.

I believe the most important thing is to realize that no minister is immune to this temptation. Flesh and blood are we still. Most ministers are great people and attractive to members of the opposite sex. Ministers have an office of respect and are seen by many as powerful leaders. This makes some ministers vulnerable to seduction and, even worse, willing to seduce others. Too many ministers neglect their families, especially their spouse. This may cause things to be less than good on the home front, making the minister more susceptible to the temptations of a relationship outside of marriage.

I guess the most important thing to say is that when you become involved in an affair, you risk everything. In the book on marriage, *The Great Marriage Physician*, my wife and I quote from the writings of a dear friend. Steve Walley, in his book *The Prodigal*, shared in great detail his affair and all the loss that followed. I strongly encourage every minister to read this book and recognize the danger of the storm. Ministers need to remember that it's a sin. Even if a minister can hide the sin from his congregation, and this is most often impossible, he cannot hide it from God. More often than not, this mistake will cause you to lose your church, your reputation, and everything you have worked for in the ministry. It can be the worst of storms!

So how do you avoid having an affair? First, be on guard all the time. Keep your guard up against anything that would appear to tempt you in this area. Don't be alone with a member of the opposite sex. Never ride in a car alone with a person of the opposite sex. Don't council alone with a member of the opposite sex. When you must, make sure there's a big window in your door and there is a spouse, secretary, or member who can be close and look in from time to time. Be careful how you touch members of the opposite sex. Be very careful how you hug, and just never kiss a member of the opposite sex. It is true that you must be careful what you say to members of the opposite sex. You may find it necessary to explain your caution to someone.

If you feel you have problems with temptation in this area, seek the help of a competent, confidential counselor. Get the help you need as soon as possible. I wish space allowed me to tell you all of the stories I've heard about ministers who have lost everything due to an affair. Be on guard because Satan stalks about looking for those who have a weakness in this area. He will devour you if you let your guard down. Just say no! This storm is like a destructive hurricane.

Storm 19: Mismanaged Storms

It is dangerous for any minister to think he is error proof. Every minister is human, and every human makes mistakes. Come on, we all know this. It's just that sometimes we think we're perfect and, worst, give the impression to others that we think we're perfect.

It may not be the worst thing in the world to admit that you can make a mistake. I have seen many congregations grow greatly in their relationship to their minister simply because their minister admitted he made mistakes. For example, we have a great idea we interpret to be the will of God. It's as if it were spoken to us directly. There's no doubt we have heard from God. Then our idea turns out to be misguided, unworkable, and for sure, not to direct communication we thought it was from God himself.

I had that happened to me several times in the ministry. I've remember working for days on a new vision only to find it rejected by just about everybody. I could have interpreted the rejection as everybody else is wrong. After some time had passed, I realized I could be wrong, and some of my ideas and visions are just mine. I have learned that ideas that come from God have more than just one supporter. He will give others the Spiritto believe also.

Some ministers also think that they just can't make any kind of mistake in life. They come across as thinking themselves perfect to their spouse, to their family, and to their congregation. How many mistakes have you made in the last ten years? How many mistakes have you made this year? If you can't think of any, you could be perfect or you may just overlook your mistakes, excuse your mistakes, and be covering up your mistakes. You can fool yourself. Ask yourself, how much do you like being around a person who never makes any mistakes and believes he or she is always right and everybody else must be wrong? An air of superiority and pride may cause others to turn away from your leadership. I have seen ministers who got off to a great start and were doing a great work crash and burn because they began to be Godlike and unable to admit any error or mistake. I heard comments like "it all went to his head" and "he thinks he knows everything." When your attitude toward yourself brings comments like this, a storm is on the horizon. Remember, God's word puts a great deal of value on humility.

Storm 20: Leadership

Everywhere you turn in the word of God, you find leaders. Leaders are people God uses to lead his people where God wants them to go. A leader leads people to be what God wants them to be. Sheep need a shepherd, and the Word says we ministers are shepherds. Let's face it; most people do very little without a leader. Every congregation needs leadership, and every pastor needs to be proactive in providing leadership. Without strong, assertive leadership, the church cannot move forward.

There are two extremes in leadership that are dangerous for the church. There are leaders who are dictatorial and leaders who will not lead. We will address being a dictator in the next section, but here, let's address the problems with being a leader who will not lead.

It has been my observation that churches successful in reaching people have a minister who is a good leader. The church has vision because the leader has vision. The church is directional because the leader has direction. The church is willing to work at achieving objectives because the leader has that mindset. This is the opposite of having a lazy leader or a timid leader. Lazy leaders don't like work, and really leading a church creates new work for that minister to do. The timid leader is one who is afraid to risk anything. He may have a fear of failure. He may feel the people will not follow, and therefore, his leadership ability will be questioned. He may be afraid he will lead the congregation the wrong way, so he leads them to circle the wagons and maintain the organization. The Church does not need a minister who doesn't have clear objectives as to where the church should be going and what the church should be doing. Churches call minister to be their leaders as well as their ministers.

Each minister needs to have clear direction himself. That direction comes from a thorough knowledge of the word of God and a walk with God. If you are walking with God and you have a thorough knowledge of what God wants the church to be doing through an understanding of his word, don't be afraid to lead. Don't be afraid to tell the church where you understand it ought to be going and what you feel it ought to be doing. If it is truly based upon the word of God, people will follow. Take the oversight! You may have opposition, but the people of God will follow. If you walk with God and he is giving you clear vision of what he wants the church to be and to do, don't be afraid to say so. Every church needs a leader!

And let me close this section by saying that the minister who will not lead is inviting a storm as his congregation grows hungry for leadership.

Storm 21: Dictatorship

We have just talked about the importance of being a good leader. In our efforts to be good leaders, we must be careful we do not become dictators. A dictator is a person who must have it their way! If there is one thing I have heard too often, it is the statement that a pastor or a minister is a dictator. That doesn't mean you are a good leader. It means you are a minister who has to have things his way, and anyone who disagrees with him will feel his wrath.

The Bible has a lot to say about selfishness and pride. This may be the problem when we must have it our way. I've heard some misguided ministers say the congregation is to obey everything they say. We excuse this tendency by saying it's not our way that we're projecting, it is God's way. But again, we have talked about the feeling that we can make no mistakes and that whatever we think or feel must be what God thinks or feels.

Most of us would agree that a husband who is dictatorial over his wife and demands that his way is the only way is not a good husband. Most of us would agree that an employer who is a dictator is not a good employer. I am sure that almost everyone would agree that a president or any other government official that is a dictator is out of line. So what is it that makes us think a minister can be a dictator and everyone will think it's okay? Too press the issue or to demand from people to obey you is to invite a storm in your ministry. I remember how a young pastor showed me a list of a dozen demands he was to make of his deacon leader the next Sunday. I encouraged him to lower his expectations and not ask so much at one time. He told me my problem was that I wasn't a strong enough leader. The next Sunday afternoon after his deacon's meeting, he sadly told me that his deacons fired him.

As a pastor for almost twenty years, I finally learned I did not have to have it my way all the time. I learned to tell my congregation and my leaders that if I got my way 80 percent of the time, I could be very happy. Whenever I did not get my way, I would say it was okay; it was part of the 20 percent. Many in my congregation and my deacons were amazed I could let things go someone else's way without getting upset about it. I actually think they respected me more for that way of thinking. Now don't get me wrong, there were some things I felt strongly about and was willing to go to the mat to get them accomplished. But at the same time, I learned there were many things that were just not worth fighting over. I didn't have to be the boss.

I guess the bottom line is how others perceive us as ministers. Ask yourself these questions, Do other people perceive me as a dictator? How do I react when I don't get things my way? and finally, Could I be a more effective leader if I were not so dictatorial and demanding?

Storm 22: Discouragement

I run across a lot of discouraged ministers. Over the years, it is amazing how many ministers I have seen quit the ministry. It's only human to be discouraged from time to time, but I think it may be a sin to be too easily discouraged. We serve a great God, and we're involved in a great work. On every hand, there are situations and circumstances; there are people and even other leaders who would discourage us if we let them. I believe one of Satan's weapons is discouragement.

I remember teaching at a conference about church growth years ago. After a rather enthusiastic presentation about the ways we could lead our church to become more evangelistic through the Sunday school, an older minister came up and told me he wished he had my enthusiasm. I ask him where his enthusiasm had gone. Thirty years later, I can still remember his response. He told me when I beat my head against a wall as long as he had, my enthusiasm would be gone also. I remember thinking, "I certainly hope not."

Over these many years, I have beaten my head against a wall many times. There have been times when I felt discouraged, but that discouragement was never so great that I became a discouraged minister. Whenever one door was shut, I would always look for another. Whenever something would fail, I would seek to start something else that might succeed. I never considered quitting. and I never became so discouraged that it affected my ministry.

My heart does go out to ministers who are discouraged. There are many who are. My heart is sensitive to that discouragement, and I would do anything in my power to encourage them. But I still believe the best defense is a good offense. Defend yourself from discouragement by being a positive person full of faith and determined to keep on no matter what. I remember Paul saying that he was down, but he was not out. I remember the word of God telling me to think about those things that are good and to keep my mind from those things that would bring me down. We all remember Elijah running away and hiding in a cave. Remember, God spoke to him and asked, "What are you doing here?" God had work for him to do, and God has work for us to do. Don't get discouraged to easily. Keep a smile on your face and hope in your heart. Keep on keeping on till Jesus comes or you go! There's a great day coming!

Storm 23: Loving People

It would seem it only natural for a minister to love people. But some people tell me they feel that their minister doesn't really love them. Is this perception reality? How can people get the perception that their minister doesn't really love them? We can get so wrapped up in leading them, preaching to them, and working for them that we forget to do those things that make them know we love them. Maybe we assume they know we love them. Maybe we don't love them as we should. Maybe we don't express that love as we should. No matter the reason, when you lose that loving connection, every church problem is a big one, and small mistakes become huge. As a result, storms that might have passed tend to hit you dead on.

I believe we agree every minister should love people. Love for God and love for others, even our enemies, is a necessity for the minister. This is very important in relation to those you minister to in the church and outside of the church. If you sense you struggle with really loving people, learning to do so should become a high priority for you immediately. People will follow you better, forgive your faults, and respond more favorably to your message if they know you love them. Even when preaching hard stuff, they will allow you to be honest with them because they know you have their best interest at heart.

Maybe a minister loves people but just hasn't learned how to express that love in ways it makes people feel loved. Much like the husband who loves his wife, but his wife doesn't feel loved because of the lack of words and actions on the husband's part. Remember the man who reminded his wife that he told her at the altar he loved her, and if that ever changed, he would tell her. He felt no need to mention the subject again. Perception is reality to those who feel unloved. You may love them but the lack of loving expressions may cause the perception that you don't.

So what are some of the ways a minister can let those he leads know he loves them?

Say so! Work at saying the words, “I love you, brother or sister” or “My wife and I really love and appreciate you.” Be friendly! Go out of your way to greet people. Don’t be out of sight before and after the worship hour. If you need prayer time, consider taking it before those fifteen minutes. Visit around the Sunday school classes before they start once or twice each week. Initiate a handshake or a decent hug! Write handwritten notes of appreciation often and keep track of those you have written so you get to everyone eventually. Make a phone call, e-mail, text, etc., as part of this effort. Be sensitive to others. Give someone undivided attention to everyone and not just your favorite people. Be a good listener. Don’t take offense at honesty or constructive criticism. Be patient with others. Contact people just to talk, not to get something. Inquire about someone’s health, work, and family.

Why not make a list of the people who need to know you love them and mark down each time you express the love you have for them. Try to do one or two people every day, and by checking the list, avoid neglecting anyone. A note, a phone call, a text message, a drop in visit with no agenda, a passing smile all say “I love you”; and people you lead and work with need to *feel* the love. Love is indeed blind, and if you really love them, maybe they will love you more and be blinded to your faults and shortcomings. This results in fewer storms.

Storm 24: Visibility

I have heard from time to time church members complaining that they never see the pastor. Sometimes they say that of some other minister in the church. I hear comments like “What does our minister do anyway?” or “He’s always in his office with the door closed!” Other comments that stem from a lack of visibility include, “He spends all his time on the computer!” and “I don’t know what he does during this time; we never see him.” As terrible as it is, I’ve had secretaries say, “I don’t know where he is.” Those are some of the comments I hear from church members and church leaders. A few of these were said of me, I'm sure. Too often they come from other staff members including secretarial staff.

Think for a minute about how visible you really are. I hope this chapter helped you analyze how visible you should be. It's important every minister has time for study and prayer away from people and privately with the Lord and his study resources. But it is also important to be seen as a people person, and the only way to do that is to be around people. It is important to be available to people for significant blocks of time.

Some of us as ministers are loners. Some of us are introverts. Some ministers really don't feel comfortable with all that one-on-one time required by ministry, so they avoid it when they can. This type minister would do well to stretch themselves into the crowd. By that I mean, a minister should trust God and force themselves out of those comfort zones and into contact with people. Resist the temptation to hide away unless it is necessary for prayer, study, or reflection. Remember, I have said elsewhere in this book that alone time with your spouse is also important, and those times should be expected. The danger is overusing and abusing any of these. Most people understand the need for study time and prayer time, and spouse or children time, but in excess, it becomes questionable. I have seen many storms develop out of the vacuum of an out of sight minister, We can spiritualize and say this is what I'm called to do, but many Christians see the work of being with people equally important as being with God. Ideally, we would be free to study and pray as much as we feel led to, but the truth is, people want to see a minister ministering among the people. Most churches call us ministers rather than monks today. So let's get out there! In my opinion, fewer storms happen out there with the people doing the ministry.

Storm 25: Angry Confrontation

Today's ministers will not always get their way about things. Things will not always go their way. I'm not sure if it has always been as bad as it is today, but evidence shows that God's servants have always endured conflict and had opposition. Think about the prophets of the Old Testament. Many of these men are to us heroes and role models. Most of them kept their cool and dealt with opposition without outburst of anger. (I didn't say all of them!) As I read the accounts of their response to opposition and rebellion, I would call their response assertiveness most often. We do see anger, but the presence of anger in these men of old doesn't make it Godly or right.

Calm assertiveness is not what we often see in today's pastor or minister. Our response may come from a lack of self-confidence, a forgotten presence of the Lord, our simple inability to properly deal with opposition, or the fact that we sometimes get in the flesh. Maybe some of us think we cannot make mistakes or be wrong, so we throw up our defenses whenever we are challenged. Too often, we take a simple disagreement or difference of opinion as an attack on us personally. Confrontation, for some of us, always brings anger. It may be our upbringing or our personality that causes us to protect ourselves through anger. Maybe our anger has served us well in the past. Maybe angry response has backed down the opposition in the past, and it has become our first option, our preferred way of dealing with what we believe is an attack on us.

Why is this wrong and why does it steer us into storms in the ministry? There are storms we could avoid with a better response. The practical reason is that most people don't respond well to anger. It either angers them or intimidates them. You should not desire to do either of these to the people you are supposed to be leading, loving, and ministering to as your calling.

The nature of anger is escalation. It moves through stages of intensity; from calm disagreement to the raising of voices; from rising of voices to unacceptable words seldom heard in a Christian setting; from unacceptable words to threats of some action or results; from threats to physical pushing, holding, or hitting. I have seen all of these levels as I both experienced church conflict personally and observed ministers engage in some type of conflict.

We should remember that anger is often included in lists of sinful activities in scripture. But sadly, some ministers find a way to justify anger. For that reason, I will not engage in that debate here. The fact that Jesus went through the temple with such assertiveness and looked in one event to the disciples to be angry surely doesn't give us the freedom to ignore the many cautions and exhortations against human anger (look anger up in your concordance). But my plea here is that ministers realize the storms anger can stir up for them. Anger never, in my experience or observation, helped resolve conflict or calmed any storm. Anger is the thunder and lightning of conflict, and too often I've seen the minister be the one eventually struck by the lightning.

If you are one who struggles with anger in church life or family life, get serious about conquering this evil in your life. Just as you conquer pride, lust, hate, and a collection of other personal sins, have victory over the anger you feel and often exhibit in the ministry. Your congregation will thank you. Your church leaders will thank you. Your spouse and your children will thank you. Keep your cool. When you feel anger rising in you, take a time out and calmly think through your feelings before they become actions and words. Allow the Spirit of God to show forth the fruit of patience, kindness, and self-control in your life and ministry. You ministry will have smoother sailing as you avoid the storms made worse by your anger.

Storm 26: Promises Broken

Life is full of promises. Promises to friends and family, to parents and children, to husbands and wives, and to people we minister to in and out of the church. How many promises have you and I made in our lifetime? How any of those promises have we kept, or more importantly for this chapter, broken.

It may be hard to believe, but I think a minister's broken promises can damage the very kingdom of God and its progress on earth. I can't help but reflect on something I experienced while in seminary. It happened as I did business with a local businessman there in Fort Worth, Texas. After deciding to purchase something costing more than I had available at the moment, I asked if we could set it up on a ninety-day payoff. His response hurt my heart and caused me some confusion. He said many ministers from the seminary had left without paying the promised payments or just failed to keep the promise of paying the bill on time. For this reason, he could not give credit to students at the seminary anymore. I guess I was sheltered or naive, but I could not believe ministers, even ministers in training, would break this type promise. I determined that day to continue what I was taught. I was taught to keep my promise of payment of debts for the sake of the reputation of ministers everywhere.

But the breaking of promises goes beyond finances. Think of all those promises we make as ministers. The breaking of promises can cause storms to arise on a normally calm ministry sea. Can I just list those that come to mind, many I've seen broken by ministers.

- The promise to call someone back
- The promise to visit a church member's friend or family member in the hospital
- The promise to get the meeting out on time
- The promise to read something given you by a church member
- The promise to a friend to give him or her good recommendation
- The promise to pass along a resume
- The promise to make a call to a reference for the search committee
- The promise to write a letter or note, an e-mail or text
- The promise to be faithful in marriage

And on and on they go, so many promises.

We see promises everywhere, and they can find their way into our ministry every day. My experience and observation is that broken promises can do great damage to our ability to lead and minister. At times, the broken promise is so grievous that it starts a perfect storm. As we have seen with presidents of our great country, promises made and broken can severely damage the ability to lead people.

So to avoid storms in the ministry or intensify storms already in progress, be careful when making those promises. Fewer promises may be preferred to more promises with too many broken. Once made, do everything possible to keep promises made. Keep notes of promises, and maybe even the date the promise was kept. Engage your spouse, your secretary, and your church staff in helping you keep promises they hear you make.

We may not get caught every time we break a promise, but the damage when we are caught is well worth avoiding. Remember, God says it is better not to make a vow (promise to God) than to make a vow and break it. Sounds like good advice in relation to promises we make to others also.

Storm 27: Just a Job

Sometimes we ministers dial up a storm in our ministry by no more than a diminished attitude or perception of the ministry itself. Church members have a way of noticing the minister who has come to see his pastor position or other ministry position as just a job.

Just a job? How could this happen? There are two groups of ministers who experience this "just a job" attitude. There is the minister who is a minister because he just chose to be a minister. It could have been the pressure of a well-meaning mother or father. We've all heard the term "momma called; papa sent." It could have been under the overpowering influence of some other family member or relative. Or maybe a pastor or youth minister who convinced you that this is what God has called you to be.

This "it's just a job" group also includes those who observed the ministry occupation and decided it would be a good occupation for any number of reasons. What I'm saying is it is easy to see your ministry as just a job when it really is just a job. It feels like the occupation you decided to pursue and settle on. For this minister, it may be exciting for a season and even enjoyable for various reasons. Maybe this minister really likes people. Maybe this minister likes being in charge. Maybe this minister enjoys, even craves, being in the spotlight, up in front of people. Whatever the reason, it is not because God called that minister into the ministry.

Now that addresses the theology of those who believe the only valid reason to be a minister is that God called you into the ministry. I gladly identify with this Bible-based theology of ministry. But that's not this chapter's emphasis; this chapter is about the attitude that the ministry is just a job. For those who are not called by God into the ministry, it is only natural that they eventually see it as just a job because that's all it really is.

The other group that develops the attitude of their ministry as just a job is that group of ministers who are called of God to the ministry but, over time, falls into this attitude that it's just a job. It is difficult to believe a God-called minister could feel this way, but over the years, many have told me they have. I may have come close to this attitude. I hope not. I'm encouraged when I remember the day several ministers were sharing together their moment of calling. It was amazing how the experience brought tears to so many as each reflected on the experience of being called to preach or into some other form of ministry.

When I went through storms in my ministry, the call of God was so strong. Once, when I resigned as pastor of my seminary church, I took a job in a warehouse to pay the bills. But I never once considered leaving the ministry. The call of God kept me focused on his next assignment for me, which I never doubted would come. Through all the pain, all the self-doubt, and all the hardship, I never once felt there was any other option for me. I believe this is the result of a call from God. It has never been just a job.

So what the point of the telling? I, and thousands of ministers, never think of our ministry as just a job. It can never be just a job because it is a divine mandate. It is not a way to make a living; it is the only way to live. We are compelled to be faithful to the Lord's will for our life.

If you begin to feel your ministry is just a job, others will notice this attitude. The attitude will show up in so many ways, and church members will begin to question your calling. This will interfere with their response to your preaching, your leadership, and your ability to minister effectively. It will also affect the passion with which you perform your ministerial responsibilities.

In time, this attitude will cause a storm in your ministry. Avoid this storm by being sure of your divine calling to the ministry. Often, refresh that calling in any and every way possible. Never spend your time in ministry as if it is just a job.

Storm 28: Stuck in a Rut

When I was younger, a well-meaning friend assured me tornados and other strong storms would not hit homes in valleys. My home was between two small ridges as was his, and my friend said a tornado would jump over our homes. Well, we never had the storm to prove this theory, and I'm not so sure how true it is. What I do know is that being in the valley or down in a rut can cause storm damage for the minister.

From my own personal experience and from hearing comments in churches, I am aware of the fact a minister can get in a rut in several ways. In some few instances, the rut causes a storm for the minister. You might think I would spend this time talking about the rut of depression or discouragement. Later in the book, I have addressed these problems and want to go another direction at this time.

The rut I need to address here is the rut that is more like the depression caused by a wagon or tire on a muddy dirt road. Most of us can remember that kind of rut. It was hard to get out of, and it tended to keep you going in the same direction. Let's apply this rut to the ministry.

The way I've heard it expressed in churches was "our pastor is in a rut in his preaching. It seems like he preaches on the same thing every Sunday." Now most of the time this may not be true, but perception is reality for most people. We preachers know that preacher comment: I'll quit preaching about it when you start doing it. But the truth may be that we got in that rut in our preaching without design and without realizing it. I can remember pastors who would start out preaching about one subject and make a beeline to their favorite soapbox. They must have really liked saying certain things or maybe felt they were at their best when preaching about a certain subject. Some seem to wander around the same five or six subjects in every sermon. I feel some guys are going to egg my house or withdraw friendship because I'm being so honest and critical. Hear my heart please, as one of you I just want to help us examine ourselves and see if we can improve and avoid the storms. A preaching rut can bore your people. Preaching the same thing over and over, even in different ways, can still bore your congregation.

Maybe we should analyze our sermons (or ask a loving but honest wife) to see if we get in a preaching rut. I remember doing a study of my sermons over a year or so. Right away, I realized there were some very important subjects I had not addressed over a two year period. At the same time, I was in a rut preaching on certain favorite things.

Other areas where ruts are common include the invitation, the way we close the service, and even the way we pray. Most agree we should spend more time planning the way we give the invitation, but it just slips away after so many hours preparing the sermon. I'm working on a book of fifty ways to offer the invitation, and it has taught me we can be creative and have some variety in the invitation.

If we will, we can spend more time planning the invitation, our prayers, and the way we close the service just as we plan our worship. Not that important? I contend it is important because I have seen this rut cause a storm. If your congregation gets bored enough or tired of hearing the same thing too much, negative stuff begins to happen. I still remember listening to a wonderful couple who loved their pastor dearly. They told me they and others were just getting bored hearing the same thing in the same way for so many years. This pastor did have to change churches because of the rut he was in. Maybe this is an argument for shorter pastorates, but I know pastors who have been there twenty, thirty years and longer and still keep people's interest by avoiding the ruts.

You may disagree with this chapter, but could I just ask you to think about it. And just try to spend a little more time planning variety into your messages, your invitation, and your prayers.

Storm 29: Church Checks

One signature on the churches' checks is a common mistake, and it won't take many lines to warn against the storm it can cause. Most churches have updated the financial guidelines, but still, some churches require only one signature on a church check. The main reason I have always heard is that it's just too much trouble to get two signatures. I could spend a lot of time here listing the many examples of storms pastors have had to weather because of this bad money management by his church.

The main storm is the pain you endure in dealing with the thief and embezzlement that can result from requiring only one signature. I have seen well-meaning church secretaries just give church money to someone they felt needed it. Sometimes, it's a needy family member or someone the secretary or signer feels is underpaid by the church. I've seen money diverted from mission causes to extra pay for a janitor the treasurer felt was underpaid.

One signature on church checks is a terrible temptation! Trusted secretaries and treasurers can get into financial difficulties and see the church check as a solution. Most say they planned to put the money back as soon as possible. You know when that ends up being, right?

Most modern pastors or other church ministers have enough on their plate without having to deal with the heartache, the confusion, and church embarrassment of a church scandal of this type.

The major storm that can arise from the one-signature check is when the pastor or minister is in some way connected to the loss of church monies. Even the innocent minister can be damaged by the rumor of dishonesty. It is sometimes harder to prove your innocence than to resign and move to a new church. This mistake of allowing your church to operate on one signature can cause accusations that follow you wherever you go or try to go.

So how can you avoid this type storm? Lead your church to require at least two out of the three or four approved signatures on every church check. Never allow your signature, or your wife's or one in your family, be one of these approved signatures. This is a little more trouble, but thousands of churches protect the church and its staff by doing so. In case of an emergency, contacts with deacons or a number of leaders can approve on a one-time basis the check with one signature. There can be a written record of the emergency approval.

Some storms sneak up on you, but this is one you can see coming from a mile away. If you and your church still allow checks to go out with just one signature, wisely change that now!

Storm 30: Mismatch

I usually address this issue with church search committees or teams, especially those searching for a pastor. But the subject is one which should concern every minister. Today's pastors and ministers face many storms; we don't need to invite another. One great storm can result from a mismatch or the unequal yoking of church and pastor or other ministerial staff. Examples of this include SBC church to non-SBC minister, noncharismatic church to charismatic pastor, missionary SBC church to Reform or Calvinistic minister, conservative church to a moderate or liberal minister, traditional deacon led church to elder-rule minister, and other mismatches. Each of these can be reversed and flipped to read the other way. These *mismatches* can cause a great deal of conflict and damage in a church and a real storm in the life of a pastor or minister. Let's not forget the impact these storms have on the family of the pastor or minister.

If you are seeking a new church in which to serve, you should do everything possible to equally yoke yourself with a church. You should seek to know everything about the church you are considering. I believe you should not go to a church so different in theology or organization than you will need to change the church to fit you.

If, as a pastor, you are searching for a new staff minister, you would be wise to know as much as possible about him or her. Becoming *unequally yoked* or mismatched with a church or a staff member is often the result of unasked questions and/or a hasty decision.

Here are some ways you can avoid the storm clouds of a mismatch. Ask more doctrinal questions. Ask about leadership style, outreach, church discipline, church organization, etc. Call people who can give you honest answers to your questions. Get honest answers from the director of missions if you are Southern Baptist and from similar leaders if you are not. Ask about commitment to missions. Spend more time with the church or the prospective minister; don't base it on just a few contacts and too little time to ask those questions that uncover a mismatch. Let me also say it is important to be totally honest about your doctrine and church polity. Don't hide anything, thinking you will work through it later.

Let's be honest. Sometimes we may be so needful of a new church position or a new staff member, so we rush through the process. You may think you are called to change the way a church or prospective minister believes or functions, but this usually does not happen. Just as a woman should not marry a man thinking she will change him to be what he should be, no wise minister would do this with a church. Trying to do so usually creates a storm. It may seem possible, but sunny days can give way to storm clouds, lightning, and thunder down the road. Just work long and hard to avoid a mismatch and the storms it can cause.

Storm 31: "Out of Sight" Members

As ministers, we have many members who are out of sight. Some of them are sick and/or shut-in. Some of these are in some type of retirement or nursing home. Some of these live at home but are unable to attend your services. These members are out of sight due to no fault of their own. As a pastor of churches with memberships ranging from thirty-six members up to over one thousand, I found the number of these out of sighters varied greatly. At one point, I can remember my list of nursing home members having a dozen or so on it.

There are other "out of sight" members who have chosen to be so through their inactivity and absence. These can number 50 percent of your membership or more. In newer churches, this number is usually lower while the older church can see the out of sighters climb to a very high percentage of the membership.

The reason I have included this subject in the book about storms is the number of times I have seen a pastor or other minister stir up a storm by neglecting these "out of sight" members. Most active members see these people as an important part of the flock. This is true to scripture. Active members would rather not judge any of these and would be slow to consider them unimportant. They don't look with favor on the pastor or other minister who treats them as anything other than members. Neglect of these members is not looked on favorably.

The worse storms arise when you are asked to visit one of your "out of sight" members in a nursing home or at their home, and you fail to do so. Worst still is that you don't go even after several requests. Active members usually give equal value to some of the recently inactive members they are concerned about. Losing members is not a good sign, so it is important the minister leave the ninety and nine to seek the lost sheep. I think ministers are criticized about this neglect more than any other thing.

The truth is we ministers should care about and reach out to all our flock, but the time required makes it difficult to avoid neglecting some. So here are some suggestions for you to consider, lessening the chance of storms that arise out of this neglect.

Take the time to make and keep updated a list of (1) your nursing home members, (2) your members who have been sick at home for an extended period, (3) all of your members who are inactive and still living locally. I found it good to keep this list on a form with columns for phone number and address or e-mail. Also on that form, I had columns to mark when I had made my last contact with each of these members. These three groups, which I looked at weekly, kept me from totally neglecting any of my "out of sight" members, especially those for no fault of their own. Having this list was good evidence I was concerned about these members and working at ministry to them.

Having this list gave me a way to keep at the unending task of contacting these members on some regular basis. Having this list to show my critics helped me silence their criticisms about not caring about these members. No matter how hard you try, you will surely miss someone, and you need to show your efforts to keep up with it. I sometimes passed this form around a deacons group to show my ongoing efforts and even enlist their help in the care of the flock.

Using this list, I could plan to visit or contact a number of these members each week. It really didn't take much of my time when I did it systematically. You may do better to set a certain day each week for a few of these contacts.

Storm 32: Staff Meetings

A complaint I often hear from staff ministers and secretaries is that the pastor holds no regular staff meeting. It seems just as bad to have staff meetings now and then. They never know when one will take place. I hear this complaint when other things are going wrong and the church leaders and some members point to the lack of staff meetings as one source of the problems.

Why are these regular meetings of ministerial staff and secretaries so important? Why do some pastors neglect these meetings? Some say they are a waste of time. Some say they just don't have time for these one- to two-hour meetings each week. Some may not know how to conduct a staff meeting. Some do understand what they can accomplish with regular staff meetings.

Even though I think this is akin to not having time to pray, visit the sick, or prepare to preach, the neglect of regular staff meetings is just as important. And this applies to every size church, even small churches with just a secretary and one or two staff members. The truth is the neglect of these meetings can contribute to a storm in your ministry. Think about it; can you imagine a football team without a huddle or a corporation without board meetings?

So what is the purpose of these staff meetings? Wouldn't this be a good time for your staff to pray together? This meeting is a good time for your staff to share the victories and the blessings of the past week and reflect on what God did on the Lord's day. The staff should work together to coordinate the church calendar. This will avoid conflicts. One conflict you should watch for is the conflict of promotional time. The events you plan need promotional time, space, and energy.

Sometimes the events do not conflict, but the promotional time and space do. Your congregation can only do so much and can only absorb so much information at any given time. You can only promote so many things at one time. Your bulletin and newsletter can only contain so much, and people do stop reading when reading fatigue sets in. The calendar update should include promotional activities as well as the events themselves. This time with the church calendar is important enough to require these regular meeting of the church staff. This calendar update should include the scheduling of vacations and other time away from the church by each staff member. I've seen small storms occur when too many staff members are gone at the same time or one is gone without prior notice being given.

Your staff will be helpful in short-range and long-range planning. It is good to hear ideas and visions discussed to make sure all the pros and cons are identified. Many staff meetings contain a devotional time. Some pastors handle this, and others rotate this activity through the staff, making sure the five- to seven-minute limit is observed by all. All the above can take place in forty-five minutes to an hour. This is a small price to avoid the storms that arise from the neglect of these regular staff meetings.

So before we leave the subject, let's look at a typical weekly staff meeting's agenda:

Five-minute devotional
Prayer needs and prayer
Calendar overview with special attention to next week and two weeks out
Look a month out to think about and calendar promotional activities
Ask staff to add to calendar any time away they know of at the time
(Secretarial staff can be dismissed when their presence is not needed)
Discussion of Sunday's activities, results, and future improvements needed
Reports of staff members

Discussion of future activities and duties related to those activities and events
As remaining time allows, sharing of personal needs and blessings
A closing prayer

If you have problems with time or the use of staff meeting time, address those rather than neglecting these important meetings. Be in control of the meeting. As the one in charge, guide the use of the staff meeting time that's scheduled. The small problems caused by this time together don't warrant the larger problems of neglecting this time together. Calendar this regular staff meeting and require your staff to attend. Make adjustments as needed. Do the meetings in a way that fits your situation, but don't underestimate the value of this time together. If events or emergencies cause you to miss one or two, don't neglect the next one or get out of this important ministerial habit. If you make it important, it will be important. Your leadership of the team makes the difference. Don't let yourself be accused of not leading because members see neglect of these important meetings of your staff team.

Storm 33: Forty-Seven Thousand Words a Day

In writing this section, I reflected on my hearing the research that says women talk more than men. In checking the fact on the Internet, I found so many studies that disagreed on this subject. Some of the studies put women's words at twenty thousand while others said sixteen thousand and thirty thousand. These studies put men's words per day at seven thousand and fifteen thousand with one study putting men's words at forty-seven thousand. This last number points to the fact that some men talk a lot more than others. So here's the connection to this chapter: some preachers and other ministers talk a lot!

Too much talking could be the thunder that precedes a storm. Our job as ministers requires us to talk a lot, but the problem is some ministers just talk way too much. It's possible the sample that included the forty-seven thousand words a day may have included a preacher. The talking problem I'm addressing is not the sermon words. It is true, too many words in the sermon can become a problem if people weary of long sermons where the preacher takes too long to get through the introduction and then cannot figure out how to end the message. Although this problem can cause a storm down the road, the greater talking problem is the number of words outside the pulpit.

Words outside the pulpit can become a problem when a pastor or minister just simply talks way too much. I remember that popular song from my teen years. It had a real catchy tune that will get stuck in your head. The song was about people who talk too much, they worry you to death, they even worry my pets; they just talk too much. Some of us fit into that group of forever-talkers. The talkative minister is one who may keep you on the phone talking all around a subject. The other extreme is one who talks very little at all. Either extreme can hurt your ministry, but the one that seems to irritate more people is talking way too much. Most times, this is just one of the many problems facing a minister in trouble, but the minister doesn't need this additional problem of irritating people by talking too much.

Just to check yourself out, answer these questions, and maybe ask a trusted friend or your spouse how you should answer these questions:

- Do I follow the person I'm talking to as they move away? (The moving away may be a hint they want to stop talking.)
- Do I often have people say they have to go or they have something they need to go do? (This is another way people try to stop the conversation when someone talks too much.)
- Do I give long answers to simple questions? (This may come from a need to talk more than is necessary.)
- Do I find myself telling so many details, I forget what I'm really talking about?
- Is it always the person I am talking to who moves toward the door or do I just as often end conversations by this gesture? (If it's always the other person, maybe you seldom want to quit talking.)

Now, please don't be defensive. My only motive is to help you avoid irritating people you lead or serve. All of us are aware of people who cross boundaries and irritate us in some way. Talking too much can be seen by many as demanding their attention longer than they want to give it. Some feel it does waste their time or it keeps them from important duties or activities. Talking too much can be the drop that sinks the boat. So as a pastor or minister, talk, just don't talk too much and cause people to wish you would stop talking. Practice the art of pausing to allow the other person to say something. Notice those subtle hints that someone gives telling you that they need to go. Learn to practice taking turns talking so that you don't notice people interrupting you as often. I also encourage you to work hard at observing and adhering to the stop time for meeting and scheduled time for conversations. Tell shorter stories with fewer details if you sense you struggle with the tendency to talk too much. Smooth sailing is ahead for you.

Storm 34: Pornography

The storm due to pornography is one of the worst. Surveys reveal many pastors and other ministers get involved in porn. When I was growing up, the pornography of the day was a far cry from the pornography people struggle against today. Today the porn is as close as a few keystrokes on your computer, your tablet, and your iPhone. There are few mistakes worse than the pastor or minister getting caught watching pornography. For the purpose of this book, to avoid the storms, I must caution every minister to avoid any contact with porn. I say any contact because porn is like a sticky trap that once it ensnares you, you have a very difficult time breaking free of it. It is an addiction of the highest order. The many pastors and ministers who were ensnared and got caught involved in porn testify to the power porn had over them. They just couldn't stop. Some would break free for a time only to be pulled back in. They risk using porn in stupid ways. Many say they neglected family, God, and the ministry to feed the porn habit or, better put, addiction.

Let's be frank and direct! If you are viewing porn of any type, stop! Don't play around with it. Step clear of it as you would a poisonous snake. You may dabble in it and one day find you are possessed by it. One slip, and word is out or the rumor is spread that you have sinned a great sin. Porn will never be an acceptable sin, nor one easily overlooked by your church. It will bring a storm into your ministry, your family, and your life. So if you are doing it, just confess the sin to God and recommit yourself to the purity and holiness you preach and teach about.

If you have avoided porn and the possible storm thus far, take heed less you fall. Guard yourself by putting protections on your computers and all other gadgets that access the Internet. Avoid porn in every form and in every place. Asking some trusted friend to ask you regularly if your life is pure, if you are free of porn or any other sexual sin.

Many of the storms we experience in ministry today cannot be avoided. Sometimes you are doing everything right and avoiding all wrong, and the storm will come, but the pornography storm is one we bring on ourselves. We can blame no one but ourselves. So avoid the sin of porn and the storm it can cause in your ministry.

Storm 35: Everything's Up to God or Is It Me?

There are two mistakes I will address in this section. One is the belief that everything is up to God, and he doesn't really need me to help him accomplish things here on earth or in his church. The second is the belief I can do it all, and I don't depend on God to get the job done in my church. Both of these ways of thinking about our ministry are based on some distortion of scriptural truth. Let's address these two mistakes as we think about the storms they cause for the pastor and other ministers.

The Lord made a statement in John 15:5 that every minister should take to heart. He said, "Without me, you can do nothing." One great danger in the work of the ministry, one that causes many a storm, is the attitude that I can do my work and do it well without a close relationship and working partnership with the Lord himself. This attitude, or should I say belief, can result in pride and mistakes. Pride is dangerous, but the mistakes we make when following our own wisdom, making our own plans, and working in our strength can bring storms upon us.

Get and stay as close to the Lord as possible. Be a person of prayer every step of the way. Personally, this is one of the great failures of my life and ministry. I still struggle with having the prayer life I know I should have. There were times I felt I was all alone in my ministry, and I believe now it was the result of not having prayed enough. I read about the prayer life of some of the greatest preachers, and I was ashamed I didn't pray more. I now believe some of the many mistakes I made could have been avoided if I had been more in touch with God in making some of the decisions I made. You must never neglect time with the Lord, and pray as much as is humanly possible. Don't think you can do much without him. Don't rely on your own wisdom. Stay intimately connected to the vine and draw strength and wisdom from him.

The other belief that causes storms is the belief some have that it all depends on God, and I just assist by being there, by being in my place. It's hard to read the commands of God and believe it doesn't matter what I do. He calls us to go to work, to witness for a reason. He brings the increase as Paul says, but the planting, the watering, and so much more depends on your hours of service. I'm really not sure how I should put this, but I have known some ministers who act as if it doesn't matter if they show up for work or not. Some seemed to have the attitude that God would get it done no matter what they did or didn't do. I believe this is a distortion of the truth that God is in control of this world and his will shall be done. Some people will die without Christ not because God wills it, but because I didn't witness enough, I didn't prepare well enough, or I didn't work long enough. I remember one pastor who told me he was bored with the ministry. After I asked him about his work, he told me a typical day was spent sitting in his office reading or being on the computer, waiting for someone to come by or need him. Our friendship was tested when I suggested he get out there where the people were and make something happen. When I told him I kept a log of the members a visited or contacted each day and that I tried to visit several new homes around my church each week, I felt like he didn't get it. Whatever the reason, he was waiting on something to happen rather than making something happen. I truly believe God wants us to join him in making things happen. Some storms come as a result of a minister appearing to be detached and or lazy. I met a pastor and his wife one morning after I finished a meeting. We were in a restaurant, and I asked him how they were doing. He shared that he and his wife usually jog together each morning. After that they have breakfast out at a local fast food place. He then said they would usually shop or swim depending on the day of the week. I must have looked shocked when he told me they liked to nap after lunch together. I don't think he will be a minister whose marriage fails, but I, with tongue in cheek and somewhat with a smile, asked him when he did work at his church. His words will always haunt me. He said, 'My church doesn't expect much, so I don't have to do much."

Work as if everything depends on you, and pray as if everything depends on God! Somewhere in the mix of these two, the good minister finds calm seas and smooth sailing.

Storm 36: It Was Just Flirting

I want to refer to a friend's book. Pastor Steve Walley has written a book about his journey away from his family and into an affair. Most of us don't realize how easily affairs can happen and what leads up to an affair. I want to share by Steve's permission out of his book, *My Prodigal Journey* by Stephen Walley. Every minister should seek a copy of Steve's book and read it out of the fear of making this same mistake. Let's look at how flirting took my good friend to places he thought he would never go. Here's an excerpt from his book:

> Enter an attractive woman with a warm smile and the stage was set. Lust was the enemy of purity. It was the incessant quest for the forbidden. Lust was the desire to have something I didn't need and to enjoy something that, in reality, I already had. It was an insult to the provisions that God had already made for me.
>
> Lust intertwines with fantasy. Fantasy could take me anywhere. It was limited only by the boundaries of the mind. Sometimes it would be

> seemly innocent as fantasizing that she would look in my direction, or that she would simply be where I was going to be. Other times it would be completely sexual. What would it be like to hold her and to have her?
>
> Fantasy could be such a tidy little sin. No one could see it. It was just me and my thoughts. Only God knew. Fantasy became instant replay. In the morning, during the day, and at night fantasy was available for my entertainment and pleasure.
>
> Fantasy would fuel my lust and then lead to flirting. Flirting was most often the first outward expression of my inward fantasies. In the early stages it was just picking at her with no apparent intention revealed. It became time consuming because it was difficult to flirt from a distance. You had to be sure that you put yourself in close proximity; go stand by her, get in line near her, sit near her, make fun of things she said or did, compliment her dress or perfume and so on. Flirting eroded all boundaries relative to safety. I would tell myself that I could handle this and not let it get out of control, but clearly it was out of control.
>
> Flirting was the last step before my fantasy made its outward debut. In my flirting, I never considered the full range of consequences. I only presumed the desired response would be the one I received. She could have responded to my advances in negative ways, which would have led to trouble. She could have responded by slapping my face, chewing me out, giving me a lecture, or even telling others about the advances. Flirting never thought about any of those consequences.

This real life account shows how simple flirting cannot be so simple after all. It led Steve into a storm that destroyed his ministry, his reputation, his marriage, and his family. Ask your spouse to hold you accountable as to how you act around the opposite sex. Avoid those who flirt with you and avoid the habit of flirting with anyone because flirting can lead to a gathering storm in your ministry.

Storm 37: Keep the Temple Pure

Every minister I know is human. We are all tempted; even more so because of our position and our influence. Satan knows our impact on others can be either great good or great evil. We can be a Godly or an unGodly influence. There are so many ways we stain the temple of God, which is our body, heart, and mind. Some of the storms we cause come from our weakness in keeping our temple pure and holy. There are so many ways that I cannot name them all here, but you and I know what they are. We preach on them often and must avoid the mistakes by being doers of the Word and not hearers and speakers only. Falling into open sin of most any kind can cause people to turn from us, and a result can be a real storm which damages the final outcome of our ministry. I have seen many a good minister have to move because of impure thoughts or actions. Once these are observed by the congregation or, more often, the leadership of the congregation, the decline of influence and leadership begins. Repentance has been known to turn the tide and still the storm, but sadly, in most cases, ministers are never restored to the past respect earned before the impurity.

Sexual activity of any type as a single minister is an unforgivable sin in the minds of many church members. Single pastors, youth ministers, and others are held to a high standard by most congregations. We have already mentioned porn of any type. The single minister's sexual life must be one of abstinence. That which we preach to the congregation must be lived by those speaking of this purity of the body and mind. Even in this generation of lower standards and more permissive morals, the minister is expected to hold the line in defense of these declining standards.

If your life has included sins such as porn, lust, questionable entertainment, premarital sexual activity, and a host of other impure thoughts or actions, and you have been *lucky* enough to have avoided discovery, clean yourself up. Don't spend another day in fear of getting caught.

This storm is one you can avoid.

Storm 38: The Great Spouse

Let's get straight to the point. Some are great ministers and lousy spouses. Both cannot exist in the same person for very long. The failure of your marriage means the end of your ministry in most cases. Sure, we have all seen some who contribute to a failed marriage and are able to continue in the ministry in some form afterward. But most times, a congregation is not as forgiving of this failure at home. Scripture puts a heavy burden on the minister to manage his house well, as an example to the flock. The minister is called to more than one thing, one focus. The problems at home arise when the minister focuses most of his energy on the church to the neglect of the spouse at home. Many spouses feel a sense of calling along with the minister, but many others do not. These spouses are there because of the love they feel for the minister. When that loving relationship is neglected for any reason, the spouse grows tired of being along for the ministry ride. Being the Christian spouse of a minister is not enough to endure a loveless or neglectful marriage. Neglect is a killer in any marriage, and the minister is not immune to the results of giving too much time to ministry to the neglect of the God-given responsibility to love the spouse and give yourself up for your spouse.

Let's be real frank for a minute and really look at how you are working at being a great spouse and, therefore, avoiding the storm that comes from a failed marriage. How much time do you give to your spouse? Just the two of you? Do you take your day off and do you give most of that time to be with your spouse? Is your spouse robbed of this day off by some activity you feel you owe yourself? Why not commit to your spouse that you will always take your day or two off and spend most of it with your spouse. He or she would surely want you to have some time to do those favorite things, but your spouse did not marry you to be alone because of the ministry and your hobbies. I used to tell my wife and children if my day off got taken by an unavoidable meeting or ministry need, I would at that time designate another day to take the place of the lost day. It was the same with vacations. My wife and children knew I was committed to time with them, especially my wife.

Does the ministry occupy your mind so much that you have ceased to be a good and attentive lover for your spouse? We've all read that stress and working too much can diminish or destroy your libido, your desire for sexual touch and intimacy. If that is happening, you are not obeying God as to your availability to your spouse sexually. God makes it clear in his word that we are not to deprive our spouse of our body when it's needed. Sadly, some minister's spouses are so starved for sexual and emotional attention that they seek love and attention outside the marriage. Whatever you feel or don't feel and for whatever reason, your spouse's feelings and desires continue. Give your spouse time and intimacy. Calendar time for your spouse, and do not let that time be robbed away because your commitment to it is weak and wavering.

So can this neglect bring a storm? I have seen many ministerial storms that arose from the minister's neglect in this important area of life. Avoid this storm by being a great spouse as well as a great minister.

Storm 39: The Great Parent

Many of the suggestions mentioned above can help you be a great parent also. And I have observed the storms which come from neglect of the minister's children. It is not easy being a PK (preacher's kid). I surely cannot be the one to tell you how to raise your children. I feel I failed mine in many ways. I just wasn't sure how strict or how cool to be. What I can tell you is I worked hard to keep them from feeling the church always took daddy away and was more important than they were. Give to your children the time they need. Structure your time and calendar to set days off and vacation time. If you don't, the ministry, which can easily be 24/7, will keep you from giving this time to these most important people in your life. I still remember the event that changed the way I gave my children the time they needed and deserved. My son was about seven or eight, and we were sitting on the couch one night watching one of his shows. He looked up at me and asked when I would be off work. I quickly said I was off today, and I enjoyed doing stuff with him. As the words rolled off my tongue, I noticed the questioning look on his face. I also looked down and noticed the open briefcase at my feet, a book in my lap, and the pen in my hand. That was a moment of truth for me. My son was not getting the one on one time he needed. I was there in body but my mind was far away. That night I decided to change the way I parented my children, and it had to be cold turkey. My briefcase, my books, my work was all left at the office. This was not easy. I even felt guilty giving myself completely to my family. Can you imagine that? No, I wasn't perfect, but I came to realize I had to really be present with my children, not just there.

Too many ministers are not even there, and many more are there in body only when with their children. Too many minister's children grow up disliking the church because it took daddy or mommy away all the time. I'm just about through with this book, and today, I observed something that caused me to come back to this spot to record my observation. While waiting for a carry-out at a local fast food spot, I saw a man, who I assumed was the father, and his son sitting at a booth. The son, about ten or eleven, was looking at the ceiling and all around. He really seemed bored for a boy with his dad on a Saturday morning. Then I noticed the dad was engrossed in the small screen of his iPhone. He was texting or surfing the web or something on the everywhere gadget we all have today. He was in another world. He was in some world other than the one with his son in it. There, that morning, I observed the tragedy of *opportunity lost*, the opportunity to connect with a child. I had to wonder as I wrote these words how many times I was with my son or daughter (or my wife) and was there in body but somewhere else in my mind. How many times did they feel lonely while I was with them? How often was I close in body but far away in my church mind?

There is a storm you can stir that comes as your children grow up without you only to forsake the church and go another way. Far too many minister's children end up pregnant, drunk, on drugs, or worse, dead in a fast car or at the end of a rope in the closet. These storms will, at some point, affect your ministry and the church you serve. The days lost in neglect of your children can never be found again. But maybe we could make up for lost time if we get started right away before it's too late.

Storm 40: Moonlighting

We are all grateful for the ministry of bivocational ministers. These ministers work two or three jobs including the ministry. Most do it because they feel a real call to the ministry and because of age, family situation, or some other situation. These situations keep many from higher education and a full-time ministry position. This is good because the need for bivocational pastors and other ministers is great today. There are many smaller churches which are a vital part of the kingdom, yet they cannot afford to support a full-time pastor and other minister.

I say this to lead to the subject of ministerial moonlighting. Scanning dictionaries leads us to simply say moonlighting is working a second or third job in order to make ends meet. The term was first used in 1957, best I can tell. In church life, this situation can be caused by a full-time church unwilling to pay enough to care for the full-time minister or a full-time minister who simply desires more money than the church is willing to pay him.

The problem is that a storm can be created by this ministerial moonlighting when the church is unaware, not approving, or embarrassed by the pastor or minister who is moonlighting. I still remember an embarrassing moonlighting job I had when pastoring one of my first full-time churches. A loving and caring couple who were business owners came to me, expressing their desire to help me financially. They asked what other skills I had, and I mentioned I was a sign painter. Soon, they were giving me orders for small signs they needed. I set up in the basement, and at night, I painted signs to supplement our income. In this case, it did not cause a storm because I moved to another church soon afterward. But I have seen many cases where the pastor got into real trouble doing what I did. I am not saying it is wrong to moonlight. The danger of this moonlighting causing a storm in your ministry comes when the church leaders are unaware and find out about your moonlighting through other means than your telling or asking them. Church leaders and church members can easily assume the minister is neglecting his duties while moonlighting. I have heard some church leaders say it is a smear on the reputation of the church for the full-time minister to moonlight, implying to the community that they don't pay their ministers enough to live on. I have heard the accusation that the pastor is too money hungry and cannot live within his means. They come to be critical of purchases he makes.

The only time I saw ministerial moonlighting cause the firing of a pastor was one occasion when the pastor tried to hide the moonlighting, and when the pastor was asked to stop, he refused. Again, I am not saying the ministerial moonlighting is wrong; only that done the wrong way can cause a storm for you. I remember one pastor who eventually weathered the storm. He and his wife sold one of those products that individuals can contract to sell. The problem came when members complained to church leaders they felt pressured to buy items. The pastor and his wife didn't mean to pressure members, but the simple act of saying "no, thank you" to the sales pitch made the members feel badly and, therefore, pressured.

So what am I saying you should do if your church doesn't pay you enough to live on? What can I say as one who has been there? Consider the salary package as you consider the call to a church. I've heard some ministers brag that they never talk money in the process of a call. They trust God to give them all they need. Sounds wonderful, and I commend this faith, but what do we say to those who trusted and didn't have enough for car insurance, decent clothes, or simply ice cream for the kids more often? I personally think it wise to know the financial facts before accepting a call to a new church. You may be able to tough it out, but consider your family and their needs and wants now and down the road a few years.

Secondly, as many do, lower your expectations and your living standards when the pay is less than desirable. I do remember the hurt in my children's eyes when we had to say no to the name-brand clothing the other kids were wearing. I do remember praying over my car each morning because I could only afford liability coverage. And my wife and I still talk about ordering a burger and apple pie at McDonald's and asking if they would cut them in half so we each have some. It was tough then, but now we look back on our sacrifice with pride.

Thirdly, if you feel the necessity to moonlight, talk to your church leadership to get their input and, hopefully, their approval. If they do, they can communicate with the congregation on your behalf if and when the need arises. And there is always the possibility the leaders will see the need and your willingness to work another job and call for an adjustment in your salary level.

Just avoid the storm that can come from hiding or mismanaging the need to moonlight.

Storm 41: Insensitivity to People's Physical Problems

When I was a young preacher, I didn't really understand people's physical problems. I would find myself frustrated when people would get up and leave during my well-planned sermon or, worse, the invitation. I remember feeling frustrated because some members fell asleep or closed their eyes while I preached my heart out. I also may have thought little about running overtime in a Bible study class or even the sermon.

I have learned so much by experience. I come to understand life better by growing older and experiencing some physical problems myself. Bladder problems are very common. Some people must get up because the urge to go to the bathroom is urgent and absolutely necessary. These people can't just hold it as you tell the children. They also feel very badly and embarrassed to do so. This is especially true when the pastor continually tells the congregation they should stay seated until the service is over. No moving around! Go before you come in, we say! But some people must go every twenty–thirty minutes or else.

Some medications are bad at making people drowsy. They often llisten with their eyes shut. Comments about the sleepers really hurt the feelings of those who are sold out to the Lord and the church but are taking painkillers in order to be present.

Added to this is the issue of saying a meeting will start at five and be out at six, and actually be over twenty to thirty minutes later. We do have lots of great stuff to share, but it is insensitive to disrespect people's other commitments, needs, and plans. When we can't find the ability to stop on time, it may show a problem with our planning or execution or our sensitivity to other people. A clock on the wall is a good thing to have and pay attention to when leading a class or meeting.

It's possible some of our members just stay home rather than feel bad about the problems they have physically or mentally. These insensitivities may not cause a storm for you, but it does hurt your progress as a minister and the overall attitude of your people. Losing members slowly because of long sermons and meetings, the minister saying one thing and doing another, or because you have been made to feel badly for your physical problems can each cause a storm.

Storm 42: Where People Sit Can Cause Headwinds, If Not Storms

We talked earlier about ministry storms of different intensity and damage. Some mistakes ministers make cause smaller storms or, might I say, headwinds. These problems may be small, but they can slow down your progress as a minister and cause ministry to be an uphill climb. We need the support and cooperation of people as we lead and inspire them. Some of the minister's thoughtless words, actions, or demands can damage our relationship with them. Now let me talk about one I was guilty of but now know the error of my ways.

Telling people where they need to sit, if done, must be done tactfully and with sensitivity. First, most people dislike being told where to sit. It's not so bad if they understand the reason. For example, please sit in areas that leave empty seats where we want visitors to sit. But to just say that everyone should move to the front because the preacher wants you closer is not a good reason to most people.

Some people sit where they sit for a reason. They don't want to be embarrassed about where they are sitting. Seldom are people told where to sit in a public gathering, right? Most people like this freedom. Some sit in a place because of social anxiety or panic attacks. Some need to be close to a bathroom quickly. Some say they sit where they sit because of loud speakers or their hearing needs. Some sit in an area because the air flow makes them cold or hot elsewhere. Some may need to leave for an emergency they anticipate or for work and they don't want to disturb or be looked at as they do.

The longer you serve people in ministry, the more you realize these factors do affect people's choice of seating. When I was younger, I just didn't think about the factors. There's something to be said for experience, right? Think about this the next time you are tempted to tell people where to sit. If you must, and those times should be few, give a good reason they'll understand and do it tactfully and as a request, not a command. True, this may not cause a storm, but who needs to give members another reason to be upset.

Storm 43: Staying Fresh Long Term

I have seen far too many pastors go through storms that ended in being fired, having to change churches too soon or leave the ministry to work in a business. Some of these storms came from the inability or the unwillingness to stay fresh over a long tenure. I've heard comments like, "We just got tired of hearing the same stories" and "He just seemed to stay on the same subject most of the time." I remember a time in my ministry when I had tried to do some creative things in my preaching in an attempt to stay fresh and interesting. The response was great, and the congregation often talked about my creative sermons that kept them interested and looking forward to the next Sunday. After that period, I must have run out of new, creative ways to present the messages. I found myself hearing a new comment. In different ways, some in my congregation said, "I wish you would do some more of those creative sermons." So I tried to change the format, the style, and the content so I did not become stale or routine in my ministry. I found it challenging to stay fresh and interesting, but I came to believe this was beneficial to my ministry. How long can a pastor or minister stay fresh? I guess it depends on the minister. What I do know is that it is to our advantage to stay fresh and even reinvent ourselves as the years go by. I've seen many ministers who seem to be fresh and interesting year after year. It's a lot to ask, but congregations do ask this in indirect ways as your years with them mount up. Avoid the storm by doing all you can to stay fresh and interesting. Consider a fresh and creative strategy including sermon content, preaching style, different sermon delivery methods that can include first-person sermons, drama content in sermon, increased visual aids, and variety of any type possible. The fact you become aware of this need will help you find ways to stay fresh and interesting. Hopefully, this will give you smooth sailing for many years.

Storm 44: Take Offs and Landings

The more I write, the more I feel I'm trying to tell you how to do the ministry. God forbid I seem to take his place in guiding and molding you. But I cannot escape the "things I have seen and have heard." Again as a ministerial staff member and then as a pastor, I remember the mistakes I made and want with a passion to steer you clear of them. As a missionary working with nearly a hundred churches, I saw mistakes ministers made that seemed simple, yet these mistakes had a negative impact on their ministries. In my effort to help ministers, I am going to risk angering you more by addressing your sermon style and preaching ability.

Some of us, when we preach or teach, have trouble getting started. Some of us have a problem finding a proper landing site before we run out of fuel. Think about it. Do you really mean to have your introduction take up half your message time? Do you chase a rabbit in your introduction that takes you away from your planned direction for the message? Do you spend four minutes telling a story that could be told in one minute? We like to think it's always the Holy Spiritleading us, but the truth is we are sometimes preaching under our own lead. But if it happens all the time, can it be God could lead you better in your preparation time. I have been in a message or teaching a session knowing I was unprepared and found easy ways to chase more familiar thoughts. There is nothing better than a minister who is well prepared and knows what he is there to say. He has planned his intro and the points of his message. He stays on track.

Then there is the problem of running out of preparation time and not planning your message's conclusion and invitation. Because we are less than fully prepared, we seem to repeat much we've said or just add stuff, flying around, trying to find a way to conclude. I remember one really sweet pastor who would preach long sermons, and his people would often complain about it. I heard him preach one Sunday, and he seemed to be lost in what he was trying to say to his congregation. I lost count, but I think he talked about every Bible story in the Old Testament before he was through. Please don't crucify me for saying these things, but I don't think he had any plan for that message. I was taught to have an objective for my sermons. The introduction, the body, and the conclusion should all move my hearers toward that God-given objective. Plan your conclusion so you don't "circle the landing strip, trying to find a way to land that sermon" as I've heard some say. Plan how you will end the sermon and stick with it. Be confident in your introduction, and let your congregation know where you are taking them. Bring them in for a landing on schedule, and hopefully, they have heard the captain speaking along the way and end up right where he wants them to be. The storm caused by inadequate preparation may be small, but who needs it!

Storm 45: What Do You Give?

As ministers, one of our duties is to preach and teach the word of God. We believe when the Word speaks, God is speaking, right. We preach in the hope that people will hear and believe. We pray they will obey the voice of God. As we preach, people expect us to be the example for them as we all obey God's voice together. Most of them do not expect us to be perfect, but most do expect the minister to be a good example of one who obeys God and does the things he preaches.

I remember the sweet lady who was helping us pack to go to a new church field. She had been one of my greatest supporters. I asked her what I could do to be a better pastor at the next church. She told me something like this, "Pastor, we all know you aren't perfect and that you have faults. But, Pastor, just don't tell us about your faults and imperfections so often. We like to think of you as perfect even though we know you are human." I had a habit of telling the congregation of my temptations and my failures. But there are some failures, few if any, that ministers will openly talk about. There are some sins and failures we know the congregation would have great difficulty accepting. You and I know what those are.

That brings me to the mistake some ministers make that causes a great storm in most cases. We preach and teach that the tithe is the Lord's and Christians should be faithful in giving to the Lord through his church. I have worked with churches who find out that the pastor or some other staff minister does not tithe and does not give faithfully. It seems this is a serious matter for church leaders. Those leaders are challenged, sometimes even required, to give faithfully and to give the tithe or above. When they discover the pastor or other minister is failing to do so, storm clouds arise. In my observations, this has always caused a storm too great for the minister to weather.

Ministers are human, and many have financial difficulties. Many times this is because the minister is living on a salary that is far below what it should be. I personally don't believe a pastor or other minister should accept or go to a new church, saying he doesn't talk about the salary. God will provide. This sounds so spiritual and it really impresses the search committee but it can come home to cause great difficulty. A minister is to be wise and plan to avoid the storms that financial problems can cause. But still, many churches do pay too little for the size of the minister's family. A second reason is that some ministers just don't manage money well. Some of us spend money unwisely. Some of us save little. Some of us can't say no to our children or our spouse.

Whatever the reason for the financial stress, the failure to give faithfully and to be a tither is a killer for a minister. If you struggle with this, allow me to make a few suggestions. My wife and I were married, agreeing on the approach we would take to our giving. We committed to writing the check to the Lord and his church first every week. We lived on what was left. If you are having trouble doing that, you have several options. You can move to a church that pays more.

But you know that is not a proper motivation for changing churches. You could go over your financial plan, even get help from some wise financial advisor or friend and budget to make the tithe your first priority as God says we should. (You know the scriptures!) Or you can meet and talk about your financial stress with trusted church leaders. Most Christians today know of this stress in every life and will possibly be caring and helpful. This is a decision you must make prayerfully and wisely. But I have seen it result in a better raise in salary, and then again, I've seen it backfire.

The decision to work on your budget and start giving God his tithe and offering right off the top is the best solution in my mind and heart. We didn't have all the things we and our children wanted, but God took care of us.

Not giving your tithe is a mistake that can cause a great storm for you and your ministry. I believe every minister can be, and should be, the example to the flock in his tithing and giving. Don't get caught doing less than you teach others they should do no matter what reason you give yourself for doing less.

Storm 46: Breathe, Body, and Beyond

Surely, I'm now getting too picky! But I could not be true to my goal of mentioning and warning of every possible danger, every mistake that could cause a storm if I left this one out. I won't say much about this possible problem and the mistake of ignoring it. There are some people who have a problem with body odor, and even more who struggle with bad breathe. Ministers are usually very sensitive to these two dangers, but I have known a few who were either unaware of the problem or they didn't think it mattered that much.

Sadly enough, the fact is that many people we strive to reach and serve are not spiritually mature enough or socially adept enough to be understanding and tolerant of a minister who has body odor or bad breathe. These people are sometimes members and leaders in the church we serve. Some are wise enough and caring enough to privately talk with the minister about the problem. But others are willing to talk behind the minister's back about his or her breathe, body, or beyond problems.

We should add that this could also include the minister's appearance and even weight. In some few cases, I've noticed a minister will begin to see his or her ministry suffer because of the distance they create or the criticism they cause. I have never seen a pastor or minister go through a huge storm because of these problems, but I have seen some whose ministry was less effective because of body issues.

So what's a pastor or minister to do? Just be aware! Ask your mate to be honest with you about these issues. Have open honest relationships with other ministers and church leaders so that any one of them would feel free and safe to talk to you about any of these issues.

When your mate or someone else does risk much to be honest with you about one of these issues, don't become defensive or angry. These issues can be addressed and improved if you become aware of them. Just don't make it impossible for someone to tell you that there's a problem. I might have already mentioned my dad's story, about him and his best friend having a friendly agreement. As teenagers, they promised to tell each other if one of them ever had bad breathe. He told me that one night he told his friend about his friend's bad breath before a double date. His friend punched him in the mouth! Don't do this type thing to someone who cares enough to make you aware of bad breathe, sloppy appearance, body odor, or weight. Let people who care watch your back.

Storm 47: Political Quicksand

This is one of those issues where I wish we could just say what we wanted, when we wanted, and where we wanted. Free speech means I can voice my political views and feelings without fear or favor. Not really true in the ministry. Well, you can, but you may find your actions and opinions cause a political storm.

In some areas of the country or world, you may only think everybody feels the way you do and thinks the way you think politically. For example, in the South, in Alabama, I think everyone is conservative and Republican or independent. But as soon as I voice my opinion to the applause of the majority, I see the storm clouds rising from those of the other political views. This may not cause a storm, but it can build walls instead of bridges between you and others in your congregation. To fight for their right to be wrong sounds good, but not really when you mean members of your congregation. People are as passionate about their politics as they are about their football. Some will pull out if you influence your congregation politically.

So what am I saying you should do or not do? Well, be true to your convictions but be wise in your expression of those strongly held views. There are ways to preach, teach, and verbalize your convictions through the declarations of God's word. Just preach, teach, and communicate the Gospel in a clear enough way that people make the connection with politics in the way God intends. I am tempted to express my political views right here, right now, but that might turn you away and affect the way you receive everything else I say. Did I just make my point?

Storm 48: To Have Passion or Not to Have Passion, That Is the Question

I've heard all the arguments for not being so passionate in your preaching and your leadership in ministry. We are reminded one of the most powerful sermons ever preached was "Sinners in the Hands of an Angry God." Read off notes by Jonathan Edwards, right? And there are many great sermons delivered in a calm, low-key voice. Some are quiet and even reserve. Others are loud and seem so fired up or passionate. Is one any better than the other?

Not really. Both and everything in-between are used of God to deliver the word of God and change the lives of millions. But with that said, I do want to say what I hear most Christians say about passion. I know I am Baptist and my circle of people may be somewhat different than some others. What I'm about to say may be tainted by several factors that may not apply to your area and your people. In Texas, Tennessee, Alabama, and Alaska, I heard people make comments like these. "I wish my preacher was more passionate about what he's preaching!" "I don't really feel my minister really believes what he's teaching." "I wish my preacher would get excited about the great things of God." These are some of the comments I have personally heard. I believe a church takes on the personality and excitement level of the pastor and other ministers on staff. If you want an excited congregation, you usually must model that excitement before them.

I know we are all different, and we each have different high limits of excitement and passion. I also believe each of us can stretch ourselves and reach greater passion. Honestly, in twenty-eight years of working with many churches as an associational missionary, only once did I hear someone say the pastor was too excited. They used the term "too animated." They told me the pastor walked all over the church preaching and was just too loud. That one time compared to dozens of times being told by someone they wished their pastor was more passionate, more animated. In my forty-eight years of preaching, my sermons were praised most when I got really passionate about the message. So what am I saying? Just stretch yourself. Get excited about what you are preaching or teaching. As one man said, "Chip some bark off the tree, preacher." I'm not sure what all that meant, but I got the feeling he was talking about getting excited and showing some passion. My personal feeling is you can't really go wrong showing passion.

As I wrote this section, I was reading a June issue of my Baptist paper, and I took note of an article about the decline in baptisms, and it mentioned the lack of passion. Honestly, I do believe a pastor or minister of any area will be more effective and be used of God more often if he or she is passionate about everything they do in ministry. Give me a minister who can't wait to wake up to a day of ministry and goes to bed looking with excitement toward another as he or she goes back to bed; as one man called this type minister, "a hard dog to keep under the porch!" Raise that level of passion, and I feel the storms will be fewer.

Storm 49: The Retirement Storm

Some storms seem to be a long way off, and they pose no immediate threat. For many ministers, retirement is not even on their radar. Some continue to hold church positions into their seventies. But eventually, retirement happens for most. I retired to write and serve Christ in new ways. Some are forced into retirement by their physical conditions or their mate's. And some storms result in the need for an "earlier than planned" retirement. I have friends going through that as I write these words.

I am always shocked when I hear our religious retirement people tell me that a great number of pastors live on little to nothing in retirement. There are many who leave a faithful mate to live on little or nothing in the retirement years after they have passed away. This can be remedied by some simple retirement planning and wise spending habits over the years. I've read that a very small and shocking percentage of Americans have any savings to speak of, even less to retire on. I was bad about this for many years and wish someone had pressed me on doing more to get ready. I know I'll make it, but it would have been nice to do better in these retirement years. It's too late for me and my wife now, but it may not be too late for you. Do what you can and more, if possible, to prepare for those retirement years. Ask your church to help you and your mate be ready when retirement comes. Many churches will contribute more if asked and if they are educated about minister's retirement. This issue may not cause a storm, but maybe, it could bring rainy days when you would prefer sunshine and smoother sailing in a bigger boat.

Storm 50: The "I'm Not Perfect, So What" Cope-out

As we come to the end of my many issues and the mistakes that cause storms in the ministry, I hope you will jot down notes of your own somewhere and even add some that you've seen or experienced. Pass this to other ministers and, hopefully, save them from a storm or two. I close with the issue of those of us who take our imperfection too lightly. Some tell me they just can't be perfect and that it's no big deal. These few seem to be in a "whatever" mode and "who really cares" attitude most of the time. "God knows the way I am, and he forgives me," they say often. Sometimes this relates to laziness, sinful activities, or personality flaws. Yes, God knows the way we are, but he is in the business of changing the way we are. I remember a couple I was counseling as a pastor. She told me what a jerk her husband was and how mean he was to her. After thirty minutes of her story, I asked the husband what he had to say. I'll never forget his words. He said, "Well, preacher, that's just the way I am." I explained to him that God is in the business of changing the way we are. Some ministers have the attitude, "Well, that's just the way I am."

The renewing of our mind and the inward work of the Holy Spiritis all meant to change our sinful and imperfect ways. My attitude, my actions, and my reactions have all improved over the years. God just keeps working on me. Every year I hope I am different and for the better. My prayer is that God will make me, with my help, a better husband and father, a better minister and church member.

What about you? Are you constantly changing for the better? Does your wife see a better husband every year? Would your children say you are always getting better as a dad? And of main issue here, are you a better minister today than you were a year ago? Don't get satisfied with the way you are. Don't accept your faults to a fault! Sure, we all are sinners and will always be imperfect, but, and that's a big but, we are told by God to strive for the perfection that is revealed to us in his word. Never preach and teach it to others and think it doesn't apply to you. Never give in to your imperfections even though they are forgiven.

Storm 51: The Spiritof Competition

I was just about to leave the section on storms we cause by our mistakes. But I asked a good friend if I had missed anything, and he said that what I now remember many others have said, even many other ministers. He said to tell ministers to avoid the feeling that they are in competition with other ministers and other churches. When I honestly reflect on my own ministry, I acknowledge I often fought against this demon in my own soul. I had to often remind myself that I am a small part of a big and glorious kingdom and that we are all in this together. Shamefully, I remember a night when I traveled to a church where one of my best friends was to preach. As I drove to the church, I remember having the thought, "I hope he doesn't do too great." Immediately my heart was pricked, and God convicted me of the pride of wanting to be a better preacher than others. I was fighting off that Spiritof competition.

We can let our pride cause us to compete with other ministers for attention, for the bigger church, or the desired position. We may be guilty of creating in our church the idea that our church is competing with other churches. This can lead to undercover sheep stealing. We try not to get caught doing such a thing. We hear our members doing it, and we are tempted to say nothing, hoping our church will grow more than that other church.

Some church members have grown spiritually to the point they recognize this Spiritor attitude of competition. They see it as one more weakness in the minister's life, and you and I don't need one more, do we? Storms can be the result of several flaws or mistakes rather than one big mistake. Too many small mistakes, which I've mentioned in the book, can do as much harm to your ministry as a big failure. Watch out for the little foxes as well as the giant in your ministry.

The Storms Ministers Proudly Welcome

Before we finish our voyage through the many mistakes pastors and other ministers make that cause storms in their ministries, let's look at those storms most ministers welcome. I personally went through some of the storms mentioned above. I thank the Lord he saw me through those storms and, as I look back on my ministry, I remember some storms I was actually proud to go through. Paul, and many other saints of the biblical past, experienced storms and opposition because they obeyed God and did what was right. Their storms did not come because of mistakes they made. The storms were not due to their sins or their wrongful actions or words. These servants of the Lord did what God led them to do and braved the storms because they were doing the right thing and speaking the truth.

Let's think, as we conclude our voyage toward calm seas, about the storms we should proudly welcome because they come as a result of our being faithful to our calling. Again, these are based on actual events in my life or in the lives of other ministers.

Storm 51: The Welcome Storm of Change

We all know that change brings pain. A survey I read years ago showed that change of any kind caused some level of anger and resistance 95 percent of the time. It seems no one likes change. One reason is humans are happy with whatever is comfortable for them. People don't like the unknown, and change forces people into unknown territory. It takes them where they have not been before. In the ministry, especially the pastoral ministry, we deal with the need for change all the time. Sinners need to change, church members may need to change, and churches may need to change also. Often, it is our job to bring that change to the church we serve. Let's look at the change we seek to bring in Christian brothers and sisters, our own church members. This includes the change they must allow or instigate in their church, which may go against many years of tradition.

This type of storm we should welcome is caused by the change we bring to the church we serve. In an ever changing world, most churches must change to stay relevant. We don't cause change for the sake of change, and the wise pastor or minister will take considerable time before pushing change on a church. Many times God has us there to properly, tactfully bring needed change to the congregation we serve. As we said earlier, don't change things too soon after your arrival, and bring the change slowly and explain it well, but bring on the needed change.

When this is the case, we should see the storm that the change brings as confirmation that we are doing our job. So avoid the mistakes we mentioned earlier in this book that cause storms, but gladly raise your sails and stow the gear, and gladly welcome the storms that come from changing a church. I had conflict in every church where I served as pastor. I guess that may point to failures on my part. But as I look back, I rejoice in the conflicts and storms because many of them resulted from my doing what I believed to be God's will. The addition of improved organization, new committees, too many new members, new building space, the reaching of people different from us, and the resulting church growth all caused me to go through storms. Although they were rough and brought pain to me and my family, I welcomed them. So if you are in the will of God, bring on the change and bring on the storms. Full steam ahead!

Storm 52: The Welcome Storm Biblical Truth Brings

I have a good friend, really several, who tell me stories of the storms brought on by their sticking to and proclaiming biblical truth. One friend as pastor was forced to leave his church because he would not bend God's truth as to what sin was. Members involved in sin can stir a gathering storm if we stand firm and strong on the word of God and call sin, *sin*. He did it in a loving and kind way. But it still angered the powers that be, and he had to eventually resign. I am proud of him. None of us should fight just to show we can, but every minister must speak the truth in love. Doing so may bring storms.

When we preach the word of God, we must preach all of it, even that which makes people uncomfortable. I remember preaching a series on the prophets, and one lady in my church told everyone I pointed straight at her and called her Jezebel. No, I didn't, and hopefully, neither would you, but the truth sought her out, and she tried to cause a storm. We live in a world where sin is a lost concept to many, even our own church members. Many sinful ways are now overlooked and explained away by Christians. Many do this because so many of our own children and grandchildren are living in sin, or what we used to call sin. If we are honest and speak the truth, no matter how loving and tactful we are, many will rise up against us.

But it's not so bad to be numbered with the saints of old. It's not a bad thing to stand with the prophets of old. It's sad to see our mates and our children suffer in the storms our faithfulness causes, but in the end, it is well with our soul, right?

Storm 53: The Welcome Storm of Church Growth

Church growth brings new people into the church. Church growth causes work and expense. It causes change. Church growth causes long-time leaders to share the power of leadership with others. Yet, if we preach the Word and go out to reach new people, church growth usually happens. Church growth is the intent of the Lord we serve and the nature of the kingdom of God. We should welcome the storms numerical church growth brings.

A good friend of mine is Ron Lewis. He is now in heaven. Back in the days of so much emphasis on church growth, Ron was a church growth consultant, and one of the guys who wrote books on how God meant us to do our part in growing the local church. We work and God gives the increase, I know! Ron tells of an experience I think illustrates the point I'm making about resistance. One night, he led his church to have a special service designed to bring in lots of unchurched people. He had a huge crowd; so many that the crowd spilled over into the hallway leading from the sanctuary. Many trusted Christ that night. Ron said he was so excited. He was really up in the clouds. The next day, some of his deacons came in and asked him to look at scuff marks the overflow crowd had left on the lower wall of the hall leading from the sanctuary. People listening to the Gospel had put their heels up on the wall and left scuff marks. Ron says he heard the leaders say, "We are going to have to paint this wall. Pastor, we just can't have this anymore!" The things you do to reach people and see God grow your church may cause storms. If so, welcome these storms.

Storm 54: The Welcome Storm over New People

Wow! I can't believe I'm saying this! New people in the church can be a problem to some! The main mission of the Church, of every local church, of the church you pastor or serve, is to reach new people. Go into the world and compel them in, welcoming them into the kingdom of God. I have always believed this was my main thing, my first responsibility. Yet in every church I served, some of the leaders and members had trouble when I was too good at this task and brought too many new people into the church.

Many of my minister friends had the same experience. I still remember the pastor who came to me after a meeting of our pastor's conference. As president of the conference, I heard from many of the pastors when they were experiencing storms in their ministry. This particular Monday morning, a good friend, who served the church closest to my home, pulled me aside. With tears and the look of disbelief, he told me this story. His church was growing, and he had been so excited and grateful over it. But as a group, his church leaders came to him after the Sunday night worship service. By the way, another new couple had joined the church that night. His leaders said they appreciate his hard work as their pastor in many ways, but he had to stop bringing so many new people into the church. "Or," they said, "you will have to find another church to pastor." He was shocked and heartbroken. He asked me what he should do. My answer is woven into the content of this book in many places. The point here is that the reaching of new people can bring a storm in some churches. By the way, my friend did find a church to serve where the church had a great desire to reach and assimilate new people.

Crazy as it sounds, reaching too many new people will bring storms for some of us. I think I have already mentioned the storm it caused in one of my early churches. The great question is with the command to reach new people, why does success in doing so cause storms in some churches?

I found some church leaders and members don't want the work and expense that comes with the success. Money being spent reaching new people seems to be resented by some. I still remember the comment by one leader of my church. She said she didn't understand our spending money to give Sunday school literature to prospects because they had not yet given our church any money. We have all seen those survey results which show a small percentage of the church members believe evangelism to be the most important thing we do. Its way down on the list of priorities for many, and pastors and other ministers who make it important enough to spend money on will experience problems with those members. I often ran into this opposition when leading my churches to spend money on outreach materials and media tools used to reach out to people.

Many members resent being asked to participate in the actual outreach efforts, such as Bible distribution or door-to-door visiting. It didn't matter that these activities brought new members into the church; they just didn't want to be asked to help. I guess they felt this was what they paid me to do. Some said that being asked from the pulpit or to have this work mentioned in a sermon made them feel guilty. I think they let this cause them to find other things to oppose and attack me about.

Some didn't like the trouble new members caused. The need for more space, more materials, or other expenses was just not acceptable to these people who felt more comfortable just maintaining the church as it was.

Then there is the problem of turf shepherds feeling relieved of power as new members come into the church. We will address this in the next section addressing power blocks in the church.

If you cause these storms by your success or even by your efforts at success in reaching new people, praise the Lord of the harvest and welcome these storms. The Lord is pleased, and this should be considered the red badge of courage in the ministry. God bless you. And he will in many ways as you do your part in the growth of his church.

Storm 55: The Welcome Storm from Breaking Up Power Blocks

As I said, one of the reasons there's a problem with new people is that some people have long-standing power and authority in the local church. That friend of mine, Ron Lewis, said so. Though he is now in heaven, I can still hear him teaching in those church-growth seminars. He would say we must realize that there are church members and leaders who have taken ownership of certain jobs or positions in the church. They have been there a long time, or they give a great amount of money to the church. Maybe they are good people who have done for years what no one else would do. Without these people, the church would have done without the leadership and support it needed in the past. But even good people can become protective and possessive of the areas where they serve. Ron called them "turf shepherds." These are those church leaders who have become possessive of some area or some decision-making position in the church. They don't like the idea of someone else, especially a new person, having power or position in the church.

We should thank God for the people who step up and serve the church in so many areas. Most of these people are wonderful, gracious, caring people. Most of these people would step aside and let someone else do the job at any time.

But as Ron said, there are some who believe, for whatever reason, the area they control or have great influence over is their own to own. They may feel this way because they have a controlling personality. Or they feel they have earned the control by their giving record or their long tenure in the church. Maybe the church has given them that position of control for many years. And then there are those who honestly think no one knows better how it should be done. Maybe they do bookkeeping for a living, so they feel they do it better than anyone else in the church. Or they do maintenance at the school, so they feel they should always be in charge of the building and grounds committee or team. These people should be highly valued and can be of great service to your church, but the danger of no rotation in any area can be troublesome in many ways. New blood and brains and Spiritare often needed to keep the church moving forward. New people can provide new perspective, new energy, and new progress, but turf shepherds don't see it that way.

The threat of a storm comes when the minister seeks to bring about change in the turf shepherd's position or amount of power. He or she can feel threatened and seek to hold on to the position. They can take it personally and direct anger at the minister. Because of their long tenure in the church, they usually have many family and friends who will take up their cause or their anger. I remember a sweet lady who had directed and served in the nursery area in my church. She told me one Sunday after church that she was tired and wanted me to find someone else to take her place. I prayed and searched and eventually found someone. I asked that person to go into the nursery and tell the sweet lady she was willing to step up and into the position of nursery leader. That hour, that very hour, I heard from someone that the sweet nursery leader was upset. I went over to the building where the nursery was located and asked the sweet lady what was wrong. She was upset that I was replacing her after so many years of faithful service. I replied that I thought she had asked me to do just that. She replied that she did, but she didn't expect me to take her that seriously and to do it so soon. I had egg on my face and much bridge repair to be done if I was to avoid a storm with her, her large family, and all her sweet little friends.

Be careful as you lead you church in changes o those in leader positions. Make sure the change is really needed. Have and use your nominating committee or team or your committee on committees to evaluate the need for change and to recommend the change. Keep yourself out of the line of fire if possible. Make sure your committee does good people preparation, notifying and explaining to them all the facts about the change.

The practice of rotating your leaders, your committees, and deacons is a good practice in my opinion. Three years on and one year off is good for everyone and gives you the chance of making changes without offending someone. Be consistent, and don't make exceptions because the system doesn't work well once you make exceptions.

One more thing Ron told his seminar attendees. There are times you must go head to head with a turf shepherd. The unruly, demanding turf shepherd may need to be kicked into the bleachers at times. Some become dictatorial and unwilling to let others have input. If possible, let others to do this kicking or setting straight of the turf shepherd. The change of these power people, though they are sometimes well-meaning people, is necessary. No matter how hard you try to do it carefully, their removal can cause a storm. If so, be proud the storm was caused by your willingness to bring about needed change.

Storm 56: The Welcome Storm over Reaching People Not Like Us

I remember those times in my ministry as a pastor when I reached out to people my church leaders would rather not have in the church. My wife and I would go visiting and reach people in the community around our church. We were younger and had no experience in pastoring a church where some members felt superior to others in the community. We, with great resolve and excitement, filled our car on Sunday mornings with people who we reached and brought them to the church. To be blunt, they were poor. Many worked for members of our church and even lived behind them. We began to sense a storm brewing when some of my leaders hinted that those people just didn't fit our church. I and my wife just kept on doing what we felt God had called us to do. I guess I dodged a bullet when I visited a black man on his porch just a mile from the church. I was determined to reach everyone on my church field. The black man told me he attended a black church a few miles down the highway. I might have really stirred up the storm if I had reached him for our church, but I lived to fight another day.

Not long after that, we befriended two children sleeping on a bus bench early one Sunday morning. We gave them a ride home and, in doing so, made friends with Mom and Dad. I eventually won Dad to the Lord and soon learned he was the town drunk. Many of my visits with him were in the local jail. He cussed like I had never heard before. I taught him Sunday school in my car because his language was slow to improve. When he finally publicly accepted Christ and joined the church, my leaders told me he would never last and shunned him. Well, this really was storm time in my church, and soon after this, I had to leave the church. I'm proud to welcome this storm anytime God gives me the opportunity to reach someone. I hope you will too.

Storm 57: The Welcome Storm Getting Organized Can Bring

A great number of pastors and education ministers know how a church should be organized. The need for committees, a constitution, and personnel policies is evident. I regret to say that every time I tried to create or amend a constitution, it caused a storm of some type. Forming committees often takes power out of someone's hands and spreads that power to many on a committee. New personnel policies change or create rules that cause some personnel discomfort.

If you need to lead your church to do these things, go slow and communicate well. Don't try these changes to soon after you arrive; be there a year or so to establish your respect and leadership. Be proud if your leadership in the needed organizational improvements causes headwinds or even a storm. Many ministers just avoid any change that would cause discomfort for the congregation. Storm or not, as the scriptures say, "take the oversight" and lead. Maybe the storm will be followed by calm seas and smooth sailing.

Storm 58: The Welcome Storm about Missions Support

I still remember the storms I've gone through because of my support of missions. In my first church after seminary, I remember meeting with the finance committee and asking where I could find the budget line for missions. The chairman, who was the father of the last pastor, told me and the committee that he and the pastor had taken that item out of the budget a year or two back. When I stood my ground and voiced my convictions about the importance of mission giving, a storm blew in. The committee followed my recommendation, and the church family voted in a budget that included mission support, but the storm raged on. The ministry there was really tough, and the father never let down on his attacks. His search for my faults and mistakes gradually added others to the ranks of his attempts to oust the pastor. I lasted about eight months there and moved on under pressure. I am still proud to say this storm was one I welcomed. The memory of this storm reminds me there are things worth suffering for and stands I must take if I'm to be a minister God can depend on. Welcome the storms caused by your love and support of missions.

Storm 59: The Welcome Storm of Deacons in Ministry

This is an area I really feel proud to have weathered some storms. I welcome the storms caused by my belief and insistence that deacons are servants as opposed to rulers in the church. I believe this is the biblical model and the great need in the church today. So I pushed for that when I was a pastor and taught that whenever I taught in churches. I do remember some of the storms over this issue.

In one church I served, there were few committees, and the deacons handled everything. Deacon's meetings were long and full of endless discussions about building repair, personnel problems, and parking lot issues. One night, the deacons shared their collective ignorance about parking lot lighting. I remember one deacon resigning in another church I served because he got tired of long discussions about what color to paint a church bathroom. That deacon told me he thought deacons were about spiritual things and ministering to the people. I felt the same.

In that first church I mentioned, the deacons were all great guys and good friends, but they just did not understand the biblical role of deacons. So I called down the storm clouds by recommending the deacons lead the effort to get a dozen or so committees elected to handle the many areas the deacons had been handling for so long. They did and soon found themselves involved in ministry to the members of the congregation. They liked it, at least most of them did.

But after a few months of letting the committees handle things, one deacon voiced a strange feeling he was having. In a meeting, he said he was having difficulty with his feeling that the deacons were losing control. He stopped in midword and said what he meant was losing touch with the church. I said, "My friend, maybe what you almost said was what you are really feeling. Maybe all of you are feeling you are losing control of the church." That night, they all agreed that this was what many were feeling, but that they should never have wanted control in the first place.

It's really funny what happened next. They decided to have each committee's chairmen come before the monthly deacon's meeting to keep the deacons aware of things being done each month. Well, the committees were functioning at high speed, so at the next deacons meeting, there were five or six committee leaders waiting to share what they were doing. Of course, the deacons felt it necessary to rehash all the decisions already made in the committee meetings and rethink the committee decisions. It took forever! With the first hour long gone and three chairmen still awaiting their turn to share their committee's work, one deacon spoke up and said, "This just won't work. Let's let the committees do their work without us needing to rehash or approve what they've done." That night, everything changed for the better for the church and her deacons.

But the change angered some, and a storm came as a result. Did I move too fast? Did I make the right change? I'm only sure of one thing. I welcome the storms caused by this important change in the work of deacons. In my opinion, you should welcome and weather as best you can the storms that result from important improvements in deacon ministry.

Storm 60: The Welcome Storm of Standing up for Fellow Ministers

I remember several times I got in hot water, or better put for this book, in a storm because I went to bat for a fellow minister. One minister I'm thinking of had been at the church longer than I, and we soon became friends. He was a good minister, and I felt he was doing a good, though not perfect, job.

Not long after I became his pastor and co-laborer in the ministry, I began to hear the negative comments. I heard he was lazy, and I heard he just wasn't the caliber minister our church needed. I went to bat for him several times and could tell I was spending some of my leadership capital each time I did. Before long, I began to hear the comments at group meetings and fellowships. I heard my friend's supporters push back against the detractors. Soon I realized I would have to take a stand one way or the other. I remembered the same type of dilemma in one of my first churches while I was still in seminary. In that earlier case, I finally became convinced the minister friend was not doing a good job and did need to be replaced. He grew up in the church and led the music even though he could not read music. Eventually, the deacons asked me to approach him about stepping down and allowing us to call a minister who could take our church to the next level musically. Bad idea! But in my less than wise and experienced years, I went to his house to talk. Surprise, surprise! Word had already gotten to he and his wife, and the loss of house payment he was getting from the church in salary became too much to lose. He attacked me as I came through the front door, and I left as the bad guy trying to run him from the church. When I reported back to the deacons, I found more than half of them had changed their minds, and they said that surely I had misunderstood their intent. Well, this bad experience may have left an impression on me, and I chose to stand by my friend and fellow minister this time around.

This didn't go well either, and my opposition grew, much of it fueled by my support of my fellow minister. Eventually, I received a call from another church while he stayed. Even today, I am proud I did not turn against my fellow minister. He was not guilty of any moral or ethical failure. He loved the Lord, and he and his family was kind and committed. I guess I would welcome again a storm that came about because I refused to throw a fellow minister under the bus.

The Minister's Spouse Can Help Avoid Storms

Before we conclude, having had a spouse for my entire forty-eight years of ministry, I believe it would be beneficial to address the storms that can come on or through the minister's spouse. Sometimes these storms come because of the mistakes the minister makes, and sometimes because of mistakes the minister's spouse makes. The attitude and actions of the minister's spouse can bring down storms on the minister and the minister's family. I have seen this several times in my nearly fifty years of ministry. For sure, the minister's spouse must go through all the storms with the minister. Let's look at some of these storms before we leave the subject and see if you, as the minister, feel it would be beneficial to have your spouse read this section and the sections that address the areas below. Another benefit of this is gaining a partner who can help you avoid the mistakes that bring the storms. A good, honest spouse can see things the minister doesn't, and the wise minister will be open to the advice of the spouse. The minister's spouse should be tactful and honest in sharing with the minister areas of concern, such as sermons, teaching, balance in ministry, interaction with people, leadership style, as well as anger issues.

Finances and Money

The minister's spouse has a great impact on the areas dealing with the minister's finances. It was a minister's spouse who used the churches' credit card with the best of intentions, I'm sure. The spouse is an important influence in the way the family spends, borrows, saves, etc. The spouse can make or break the minister in the financial area. This is a good place to praise my spouse of forty-eight years. She never complained about the house we had to live in. She seldom asked for anything we could not afford without going into large debt. She helped me live within our means and was a supporter of our commitment to the tithe even in the tough times we went through. Some ministers I have known talked about the pressure to move to a larger church because of pressure from a spouse instead of the call of God. Your spouse can truly be a helpmate or a troublemaker in this important area of finances.

Morality and Ethics

It is vitally important the minister's spouse have and sustain a good moral compass and keep his or her life morally and ethically pure. It saddened me whenever I saw a minister's spouse fall into the trap of an affair, or get involved in porn, or be found lying about something, or misusing church money. There are several sections the minister should read to a spouse or ask the spouse to read. I actually believe it would be greatly beneficial for the spouse to read this entire book. The moral failure of the minister's spouse can greatly damage the work of the minister. Church people seem to be more judgmental toward the minister's spouse than toward the children or actually anyone else.

Loving People

Many a minister's spouse deals with the struggle to be a people person. As with the minister, the spouse needs to be comfortable with people and be able to show love and appreciation for the people in the congregation and those the congregation reaches out to. As I said, this can be an area where personality makes it hard, but most of us can improve in this area if we really try with the help we allow God to give us. If this is a difficult area, stretch yourself and let your love for people and the Lord overcome the urge to avoid people. A good counselor can help in this area.

Anger and Abuse

Anger and abuse of some type by the minister's spouse can be a problem because we are all human. My wife and I can testify to the truth that we all, as ministers and spouses, have our own struggles and our own demons to fight against. We worked through some anger issues and were able to overcome them before they destroyed our marriage and our ministry. We also have knowledge of many minister's homes where anger and abuse was a great threat. It still amazes me that ministers and minister's spouses can be abusers, the ones who, behind closed doors, act in a totally unacceptable way. But experience taught me this is the case in many minister's homes. The minister's spouse must avoid the presence of angry outburst and/or abuse of any kind, just as I said of the minister. The minister's marriage and family is expected to be the example to follow and not the example to avoid. If anger is a common experience in your home, deal with it before it brings a greater storm into your ministry.

Criticism and Opposition

The need to properly deal with criticism and opposition is as important for the minister's spouse as it is for the minister. If the minister's spouse demonizes those who are critical, it makes it harder for the minister to manage these people properly. This can also pose a threat to the minister's relationship with the spouse. For this reason, the wise minister will spend time and energy teaching the spouse and the children how to view and treat those who are critical. The opposition must be loved, not hated. I think Jesus had a lot to say about that, didn't he? I have seen great storms caused by a spouse who says the wrong thing in anger or refuses to love the enemy as well as the supporters.

Spouse's Tongue

This brings me to the issue of the spouses tongue. We addressed this in the minister's life, and it would do us all good to consider the tongue of the spouse. By tongue, I mean the things the spouse says and the way the spouse says those things. And I should add, where the spouse says the things he or she wants to say. As with the minister, the spouse can talk too little or too much. If the spouse talks too little or has difficulty carrying on a conversation, the congregation could feel the spouse is unhappy with the ministry or the church. The spouse's personality can be such that easy interaction with people is difficult and even stressful. If this is the case, the spouse can simply acknowledge the problem and stretch his or her talking skills to talk more comfortably. In extreme cases, counseling could prove helpful and eventually reduce the stress and the possible difficulties he or she has a part of the ministry team.

Then, there's the spouse who talks too much. I remember as a teenager the popular song "You Talk Too Much." We talked earlier about the minister who talked too much, and it could be a problem for the spouse also. As with the minister, the overly talkative spouse can irritate people or frustrate them. This is most likely a personality disorder. Some people talk excessively because of anxiety. Others like the feeling of being in control of the conversation. Others live in a self-centered universe where all that matters is what the talker thinks. It can be a need to control others. It may be that talking is the only way a spouse feels noticed or important. The talker has little interest in listening to the other person and talks excessively to shut the other person down. The spouse who talks too much can simply be a good storyteller and enjoy telling all the details. Sometimes this slips into chasing rabbits and may become boring to the listener who, by the way, might have something to say. Whatever the reason, talking too much can be a problem and needs to be acknowledged and adjusted.

Worse than talking too much or too little, the spouse can easily betray a confidence or join into the latest gossip. This seems a small thing, but trust me when I say it can cause storms of different intensity if the spouse doesn't guard the tongue. Over and over, I have heard the minister criticized for the things the spouse has said. There is a time to speak and a time to be silent as the Word says. In spite of the feeling I'm being too hard on the minister's spouse, I have seen the spouse make a difference between the success and failure of the minister. A minister's spouse who has a temper or speaks whatever he or she feels before thinking about the way it comes across will be a storm-causing spouse. This has been my observation over the years. As a minister's spouse, watch your conversation. Watch the things you say and to whom you say it! Stay in control of your temper and be careful to whom you show your anger. Please hear my heart. I know the ministry is not easy, and it is often unfair. I am sorry the church doesn't always act in love and compassion toward the minister and family, but the church family needs to see one good example of loving the enemy and blessing those who persecute. The minister's spouse can be that example for the congregation to see. It's also good for the unchurched to see this example.

Flirting

Then there is the problem of the minister's spouse and flirting. I'm talking about the flirt that should not be given or the flirt that should not be received. Just as the minister guards against the temptation to flirt or to be the victim of the flirtatious person, the spouse must do the same. The spouse must avoid every appearance of evil. Don't touch a person you are close to because the touch can be interpreted as some advances you do not intend. Don't be alone or in a private setting with someone where that can leave you open to an accusation that you have not defense against. Sadly enough, you can be innocent yet wrongly judged so easily. My wife and I noticed there were sweet people who had feelings for her or me, and we both had to be on guard less one of us falls prey. So guard your heart but also guard your actions.

Time with the Minister

Now let's think together about the time you have with the minister you married. The spouse deserves the appropriate time to be with the minister away from the job. The spouse can help the minister avoid storms by encouraging the minister to honor the time off given and guard the vacation time for both the minister's sake and the minister's family. But a proper warning for the minister's spouse is that he or she must not put pressure on the minister for time not given by the church or organization. Many times I have seen a spouse demand time the minister does not have and find ways to draw the minister away from his or her assigned duties. A needy spouse can cause a minister to take time away from the job and even to the neglect of the sick and the lost. I regret the demands of the minister are great and, for that reason, encourage every minister to take time off and vacation time very seriously and not deprive the spouse or family of that well-deserved time. But a needy spouse can create stress on the minister and a negative impression from the church leadership and members. Too much demand or intrusion by the minister's spouse can do great harm.

Discouragement

The minister's spouse must avoid the many fruits of discouragement. An unhappy spouse or a discouraged spouse can weigh heavy on the minister. This problem can affect the congregation as well as the minister. The spouse should be careful not to become isolated from others and appear as one who does not like the church. We've all heard the saying, "If mother is not happy, nobody's happy." Many a minister's spouse has a difficult life at best, and I regret that the life of the minister's spouse and family can be so hard. But with that said, how well the spouse and the family deal with the difficulties often determines how long the minister can effectively minister at any given church or religious organization.

Welcoming the Good Storms

Finally, I must encourage the minister's spouse to understand that many storms are the result of the minister's faithful obedience to God's call and doing things that God leads the minister to do. Even though the storm is not due to a mistake the minister made, it can be no less painful. It is so important the spouse support the minister when storms come due to the minister's faithful service to the church and to God.

Whatever problem the minister's spouse deals with, it must not be swept under a rug but recognized and addressed properly. The minister and spouse are a team, and what affects one affects the other. Counselors, other ministers and spouses, and good wise friends can all help the minister's spouse avoid the storms that do damage to so many others. My prayer is that God bless both the minister and the spouse as their years of service continue together.

Conclusion: The Minister Mariner's Prayer for Calm Seas and Fair Skies

Dear Lord, you are the Lord of the universe and Lord of your church. As your willing servant, I need your wisdom that helps me steer clear of those mistakes, personal habits, and traits that can bring storms into my ministry. I welcome the storms resulting from my faithfulness. I commit myself to allowing you to change me in any way you choose. Make me of more benefit to your kingdom's growth. Be with me and my family as we sail through the storms of ministry. Minimize the damage done by the storms and keep me sailing in calm seas with your winds at my back until safely in your harbor in Jesus's name. Amen.

Monthly Storm Avoidance Checkup for Display

___ I will not use church credit card for any personal or family purchases.
___ I will pray a long time and think twice.
___ I will not deprive my family of vacation or off days.
___ Good organization is important to me.
___ I will work to keep my ministry and my preaching balanced.
___ I will love and treat respectfully those who oppose me.
___ I will welcome and seek to benefit from criticism.
___ I will not demonize those who oppose me.
___ I will be very, very careful in my use of church money and/or expense allowances.
___ I will find a way to express appreciation to at least one person each workday.
___ I will work the hours expected of me, never allowing anyone to see me as lazy
___ I will not flirt, act or speak inappropriately, or be alone with someone of opposite sex.
___ I will minister as a leader of the church and never as a dictator.
___ I will be visible out there where the people are *rather than* always at my desk.
___ I will stay in control of my anger and be assertive in love instead.
___ I will be careful as to promises I make and keep promises made.
___ My ministry is not just a job; it is God's call on my life.
___ I will lead my church to have approved financial safeguards, including two signers on checks, and two counters for all monies, along with receipts on all expenditures.
___ I find ways and time to stay in contact with "out of sight" members.
___ Because I see value in staff meetings, I will have staff meeting on a regular basis.
___ I will not talk too much or too little.

___ I refuse to risk everything by viewing pornography.

___ I will not depend totally on my work alone nor on God's work alone; therefore, I will do all I can while God does all he will.

___ I will always make time to be a good spouse.

___ I will also find time to be a good parent to my children.

___ I will be sensitive to people's physical and emotional problems as I make decisions.

___ I will make my best effort at being a people person, showing love to everyone.

___ I will work at staying fresh throughout my entire ministry.

___ I strive to prepare better sermon beginnings and endings.

___ I commit myself to being a good example of tithing and sacrificial giving.

___ Though never perfect, I will always strive to be perfect for my Lord.

___ I will be as passionate as possible for as long as possible in my ministry.

Other ideas I add for smooth sailing in my ministry:

About the Author

Jerry was called into the ministry at age twenty and served churches for forty-nine years. He just retired from twenty-eight years of service as the associational missionary for the Tuscaloosa County Baptist Association. During this time, he worked with eighty-seven churches and more than four hundred pastors and other ministers. Before that, he served as pastor of churches in Texas, Tennessee, and Alabama. Jerry is a graduate of Southwestern Baptist Seminary and Samford University. Wilkins traveled extensively leading conferences on church outreach and growth. Other books include *Marketing Your Sunday School, A Practical Guide to Associational Missions, Let God Speak When Conflict Arises, and The Great Marriage Physician.* He has been married to Carole for forty-eight years, and they have two grown children and one grown granddaughter. Both Jerry and Carole have authored several books together and continue to write in retirement while serving in their local church.

CPSIA information can be obtained at www.ICGtesting.com
Printed in the USA
LVOW11s0800080315

429627LV00001B/60/P

9 781634 173940